WINNING THE
LONG WAR

WINNING THE LONG WAR

RETAKING THE OFFENSIVE AGAINST RADICAL ISLAM

Ilan Berman

With a Foreword By
The Honorable Newt Gingrich

ROWMAN & LITTLEFIELD PUBLISHERS, INC.
Lanham • Boulder • New York • Toronto • Plymouth, UK

Published by Rowman & Littlefield Publishers, Inc.
A wholly owned subsidiary of The Rowman & Littlefield Publishing Group, Inc.
4501 Forbes Boulevard, Suite 200, Lanham, Maryland 20706
http://www.rowmanlittlefield.com

Estover Road, Plymouth PL6 7PY, United Kingdom

British Library Cataloguing in Publication Information Available

Library of Congress Cataloging-in-Publication Data

Berman, Ilan.
    Winning the long war : retaking the offensive against radical Islam / Ilan
Berman.
        p. cm.
    Includes bibliographical references and index.
    ISBN 978-0-7425-6619-4 (cloth : alk. paper) — ISBN 978-0-7425-6621-7
(electronic)
    1. Terrorism—Prevention. 2. Terrorism—Religious aspects—Islam. 3.
Radicalism—Religious aspects—Islam. I. Title.
    HV6431.B479 2009
    363.325'16—dc22

                                                    2009009257

∞ ™ The paper used in this publication meets the minimum requirements of
American National Standard for Information Sciences—Permanence of Paper
for Printed Library Materials, ANSI/NISO Z39.48-1992.
Printed in the United States of America

For Lauren,
The other reason why I fight

CONTENTS

FOREWORD by The Honorable Newt Gingrich   ix

ACKNOWLEDGMENTS   xi

INTRODUCTION   xiii

  1   **FIGHTING SMARTER**   1

  2   **WANTED: AN IDEOLOGICAL OFFENSIVE**   11

  3   **MESSAGING TO THE (MUSLIM) MASSES**   31

  4   **ECONOMIC AREA DENIAL**   51

  5   **WEAPONIZING INTERNATIONAL LAW**   75

  6   **STRATEGIC DEMOCRATIZATION**   93

CONCLUSION   115

INDEX   119

ABOUT THE AUTHOR   125

FOREWORD

The fight against radical Islam is, unfortunately, certain to continue for years. Our armed forces are stretched to their limit, short on personnel, and in need of recapitalization. Our military commanders in Afghanistan have requested additional troops that we are hard-pressed to provide. Our military commanders in Iraq, understandably, are reluctant to give up the troops they have, lest they lose the gains that have been made there. If we are to stem the tide of Islamic radicalism, then we must do more than simply continue down the path we are currently on. We will need to reshape the strategic environment itself.

In fighting the enemies we face today and those we may face tomorrow, success lies in focusing all aspects of our national power. There has been much negative commentary lately directed at those who have said that we cannot simply shoot our way to victory. Some have even suggested that those who hold that belief are defeatists. Such foolish criticisms reflect a lack of familiarity with the art of war. As the great strategist Carl von Clausewitz made clear, victory ultimately depends upon a political solution. A whole-of-government approach is essential in any conflict—and especially to one against an irregular, ideological enemy.

Make no mistake: the future is as unpredictable today as it ever has been. We face an enemy that has publicly stated its commitment to our destruction. We cannot rest on our laurels and hope that the future will be free of violence. Human nature tells us otherwise. We must maintain a strong defense and clearly communicate to those who would bring harm to us what the costs will be should they choose to do so.

Radical Islamists brought the fight to our shores. We must end it on theirs. Ilan Berman provides a thought-provoking and convincing argument for the challenges we face in the "Long War," how we have missed the mark in our prosecution of it so far, and the next steps we must take to achieve victory. His analysis is forward thinking, insightful, and lucid. Radical Islamists are mobilizing against the West, and we are failing to meet the challenge. Since September 11, 2001, we have made critical errors. But so have our enemies. Every crisis is also an opportunity, and Ilan Berman presents clear solutions that—if acted upon today—will not only change the course of the current fight but can also hasten the end of radical Islamism once and for all. *Winning the Long War* is a seminal call to action that should be required reading for all national security practitioners and each citizen of the United States. If we act upon its message, we most certainly can retake the offensive against radical Islam.

The Honorable Newt Gingrich
Former Speaker of the
U.S. House of Representatives

ACKNOWLEDGMENTS

In many ways, the seeds for *Winning the Long War* were sown on September 11, 2001. For anyone watching on that day, it was abundantly clear that the terrorist attacks on New York and Washington, DC, had catapulted the United States into a grave new world. In the years since, America has slowly begun to define, and stake its claim to, this *terra incognita*. This book is my humble attempt—drawn from more than a decade of professional work in foreign policy and national security analysis—to synthesize what we have done right in this conflict so far, what we have not, and the great many things that still remain to be done.

As always, I am deeply indebted to American Foreign Policy Council (AFPC) president Herman Pirchner. During my eight years at AFPC, he has served simultaneously in many roles: a good friend, a wise mentor, a fierce critic, and a staunch advocate. It is in no small measure thanks to him that I have had the both the opportunity and the temerity to tackle so daunting a project.

But I did not do so alone. A great many people share the credit for this effort. Jeff Smith, Rich Harrison, Hillary Downs, Adam Farrar, and Matt Brodsky all provided indispensable assistance on various aspects of this book. Their input—as well as their intellectual curiosity and their own respective areas of expertise—have had a profound impact on the final product.

So have those of policy experts whose knowledge of the topics covered herein dwarfs my own. Jim Robbins, Paul Janiczek, Bob Reilly, Bob Schadler, Eric Clark, Roger Robinson, Andrew Davenport, and Adam

Lovinger, as well as a great many others who by necessity must remain nameless, all lent their eyes, their ears, and their formidable intellects to this enterprise. They have my heartfelt thanks for doing so.

Two other people deserve special mention. The first is Liz Wood, AFPC's fantastic in-house editor, whose absolute mastery of the English language has helped my writing immeasurably on this and so many other occasions. The second is my agent, Don Gastwirth, who has been a tireless champion of my work since the day we met, and who believed in this project even during the times when I did not.

My biggest debt, however, is without a doubt to my family, which has provided me with both the inspiration and the support to make this work a reality. Over the years, my wife Hillary has grown accustomed to the long absences—both intellectual and physical—that stem from my work, and borne them all with a grace and patience that I could not have hoped for. And while my children, Mark and Lauren, are still too young to read this book, it is my sincere hope that one day, when they do, it will help them understand the scope of the current struggle—and appreciate why failure is simply not an option.

INTRODUCTION

A re we winning what, at least until recently, was known as the War on Terror? Nearly a decade after the September 11 attacks, and in the wake of two wars in the greater Middle East, there is cause for cautious optimism.

As of this writing, conditions in Iraq have unmistakably turned a corner, thanks in no small measure to the "surge" strategy adopted by the Bush administration in 2007. Some two years on, that approach has shifted the tide of battle decisively away from al-Qaeda and the insurgency in the favor of the United States and its Coalition partners. According to U.S. intelligence officials, al-Qaeda in Iraq is now "near total defeat," progressively dismantled by Coalition forces and routed by an "awakening" of local Sunni tribes that have rejected the organization's vision for their country.[1] And al-Qaeda is not the only one. Increasingly, Iraq's various sectarian militias are also on the defensive, squeezed by an assertive, nationalist Iraqi central government determined to establish order throughout the country.

U.S. military officials have been quick to warn that these gains are still fragile and "reversible."[2] But more than a few observers, surveying the dramatic transformation that has taken place in the former Ba'athist state, have concluded that, for all the challenges that still remain, the war there is now effectively won.[3]

By contrast, America's gains on the struggle's first front, Afghanistan, are a good deal more tenuous. The Taliban remains a dogged and dangerous adversary—one that is now being reinforced by foreign fighters fleeing the battlefield in Iraq for greener pastures.[4] The country's police force, a key building block of domestic stability and postconflict reconstruction, remains unfocused and riddled with corruption.[5] Its tempestuous politics, meanwhile, are still prone to upheavals and fractious power struggles.[6]

If one takes the longer view, however, the trend line has been unequivocally positive. "Until the US-led invasion in 2001, Afghanistan was the cockpit of ascendant Islamist terrorism," British commentator Gerard Baker points out. "Between 1998 and 2005 there were five big terrorist attacks against Western targets. . . . All owed their success either exclusively or largely to Afghanistan's status as a training and planning base for al-Qaeda." But "[i]n the past three years there has been no attack on anything like that scale"—a fact attributable in no small part to the elimination of Afghanistan as a key terror haven.[7] And with a renewed American commitment to victory, manifested in the Obama administration's initial decision to deploy an additional 17,000 combat troops to help secure Afghanistan, there is real hope that Washington will be able to break the "stalemate" now confronting Coalition forces there.[8]

At home, meanwhile, the U.S. government has embarked upon the single largest strategic reorientation in over half a century. In the days immediately after September 11, President George W. Bush pledged to the American people that he would confront and defeat the terrorist threat that had declared war upon the United States. In the years that followed, his government undertook a profound transformation of national security. It established the free-standing Cabinet-level Department of Homeland Security tasked with predicting, preventing, and mitigating future terrorist attacks on American soil. It passed sweeping—albeit controversial—provisions granting law enforcement agencies greater power to monitor, investigate, and apprehend suspected terrorists, and eliminated the notorious bureaucratic "Chinese wall" that in previous years had complicated and discouraged communications between government agencies tasked with domestic law and order and those focused on the gathering of foreign intelligence. And it launched groundbreaking new international efforts designed to counter global proliferation and better defend American allies abroad.

Cumulatively, these changes are comparable in scope and reach to the National Security Act signed by President Harry Truman in 1947, which restructured the U.S. military, intelligence community, and national security decision-making apparatus in order to better fight the

Cold War. Because of them, Americans can take comfort in the fact that they are much safer today than they were on September 10, 2001.

When it comes to the larger struggle against radical Islam, however, the United States is faring considerably less well. We have failed to keep pace with al-Qaeda's metamorphosis from a terrorist group into a global ideological movement, or to take advantage of its latent operational, economic, and political vulnerabilities. We have steadily drifted toward accommodation with the radical revolutionary regime in Iran, the world's leading state sponsor of terrorism. And we have fallen short in formulating a cogent and compelling message to the Muslim world about why the vision of our extremist opponents is destructive and dangerous, to them and to us. Indeed, the United States today gives every indication of losing the initiative in the struggle against the forces of radical Islam.

This drift can be chalked up to two principal problems—one conceptual, the other strategic.

The first involves a failure to properly identify our adversaries. Such a step seems eminently intuitive. After all, you can't fight an enemy whose characteristics you do not know. And yet, that is precisely what the United States has been doing for the past seven-and-a-half years.

At its core, the problem is not one of terminology. To be sure, many have argued that the War on Terror is a misnomer, since "terrorism" is simply a tactic used by radicals to advance their agendas. As President Bush himself famously put it back in 2004: "We actually misnamed the war on terror, it ought to be the struggle against ideological extremists who do not believe in free societies who happen to use terror as a weapon to try to shake the conscience of the free world."[9] More recently, the Obama administration has opted to scrap the phrase entirely in favor of the more anodyne "Overseas Contingency Operation" in its official speeches and pronouncements.[10] In practice, however, both the United States and its adversaries understand full well the objective of the current struggle: to confront and defeat the forces of radical Islamic extremism.

Rather, the challenge is one of focus. Since September 11, the current conflict has been defined too narrowly, as principally a struggle against al-Qaeda and its fellow travelers. As a result, America has given little thought to how it can successfully confront and defeat others that may operate differently or to engage the silent Muslim majority that will determine whether our adversaries succeed or fail in their efforts.

The second has been an inability to identify, and then to dominate, the real battlefields of the War on Terror. As the experiences of the past decade-and-a-half in the Persian Gulf, the Balkans, and Southwest Asia have shown all too clearly, the armed forces of the United States quite simply have no equal. But, precisely because of this brilliance, America is now in danger of succumbing to the old adage that "when you have a hammer, everything looks like a nail." Our successes on the battlefield in places like Afghanistan and Iraq have led more than a few observers to conclude that the current conflict can be won predominantly by force of arms.

Nothing could be further from the truth. The U.S. military does indeed have a critical role to play in the fight against violent Islamic extremism. But the sheer size of our adversary indicates that the military should not—indeed, cannot—be the tip of the spear in our struggle.

There are encouraging signs that policymakers in Washington have begun to grasp this reality. As Secretary of Defense Robert Gates famously explained, the current conflict in which the United States has found itself "cannot be overcome by military means alone." Rather:

> [It] will be fundamentally political in nature and will require the integration of all elements of national power. Success to a large extent will depend less on imposing one's will on the enemy or putting bombs on target—though we must never lose our will or ability to unsheathe the sword when necessary. Instead, ultimate success or failure will increasingly depend more on shaping the behavior of others—friends and adversaries, and most importantly, the people in between.[11]

As a practical matter, however, the U.S. government has been slow to shift focus. In what defense planners term the "nonkinetic" areas of the current conflict—ideology, strategic influence, economic warfare, international law, and democracy promotion—the United States can and should be doing much more. After all, it is these fronts, and not the military ones, that are likely to be our principal battlegrounds in the years ahead. Our adversaries know full well that they are no match for U.S. forces in conventional terms. Their only hope is to outflank and out-think the United States in terms of politics and ideology. And so far, the United States has been allowing them to do just that. Washington has already achieved dominance on the military battlefield of the current struggle. Now it needs to do the same on the political, economic, and legal ones.

This book is about those gaps in current American counterterrorism strategy, and what the United States will need to do in order to close them. It is also about the need for more creative thinking about the nature of the conflict in which the West now finds itself, and the road ahead. Most of all, it is about how the United States and its allies can retake the offensive in what has become the defining struggle of our time.

NOTES

1. CIA Director Michael Hayden, as cited in Joby Warrick, "U.S. Cites Big Gains against Al-Qaeda," *Washington Post*, May 30, 2008, http://www.washingtonpost.com/wp-dyn/content/article/2008/05/29/AR2008052904116_pf.html.

2. See, for example, "General Odierno Warns Gains in Iraq Reversible," msnbc.com, September 16, 2008, http://www.msnbc.msn.com/id/26733319.

3. See, for example, Bing West, "The War in Iraq Is Over. What Next?" *Wall Street Journal*, August 12, 2008, A21.

4. Pamela Hess, "Ambassador: Al-Qaida Leaving Iraq for Afghanistan," Associated Press, July 23, 2008, http://news.yahoo.com/s/ap/20080724/ap_on _go_ca_st_pe/al_qaida_afghanistan_4.

5. See, for example, "Policing Afghanistan: Still Searching for a Strategy," International Crisis Group *Asia Briefing* 85 (December 18, 2008), http:// www.crisisgroup.org/library/documents/asia/south_asia/b85_policing_in _afghanistan_still_searching_for_a_strategy.pdf.

6. See, for example, James S. Robbins, "Afghanistan: Back to Basics," *The Journal of International Security Affairs* 15 (fall 2008).

7. Gerard Baker, "Cheer Up. We're Winning this War on Terror," *Times of London*, June 27, 2008, http://www.timesonline.co.uk/tol/comment/columnists/ gerard_baker/article4221376.ece.

8. "U.S. Commander: Troops 'Stalemated' in Afghanistan," Associated Press, February 18, 2009, http://www.msnbc.msn.com/id/29270777.

9. As cited in Dana Milbank, "Reprising a War with Words," *Washington Post*, August 17, 2004, http://www.washingtonpost.com/wp-dyn/articles/ A6375-2004Aug16.html.

10. Scott Wilson and Al Kamen, "'Global War on Terror' Is Given a New Name," *Washington Post*, March 29, 2009, http://www.washingtonpost.com/wp-dyn/ content/article/2009/03/24/AR2009032402818.html.

11. Secretary of Defense Robert M. Gates, Remarks at the Air War College, Maxwell, Alabama, April 21, 2008, http://www.defenselink.mil/speeches/ speech.aspx?speechid=1231.

1

FIGHTING SMARTER

With whom are we at war? On the surface, the answer seems obvious. It was Osama bin Laden who, in his now-famous 1998 fatwa, declared "kill[ing] the Americans and their allies—civilians and military" to be "an individual duty for every Muslim."[1] Three years later, bin Laden made good on his threat when his organization, al-Qaeda, carried out the bloodiest terrorist attacks in American history, killing more than three thousand civilians in New York, Washington, DC, and rural Pennsylvania.

To a large degree, American strategy has conformed to this conventional wisdom.[2] From the very start, the United States has been waging the War on Terror chiefly on the Sunni side of the religious divide within Islam. The principal targets have been al-Qaeda and its affiliates, such as the Taliban in Afghanistan and Sunni insurgents in Iraq. Thus the White House's most recent counterterrorism strategy, issued in September 2006, focuses overwhelmingly on the bin Laden network and its fellow travelers, which are seen as the vanguard of "a transnational movement of extremist organizations, networks, and individuals" threatening the United States.[3] To a large extent, so does the Pentagon's 2008 National Defense Strategy, which declares that "[w]e face an extended series of campaigns to defeat violent extremist groups, presently led by al-Qaeda and its associates."[4]

Delve a bit deeper, however, and the situation becomes more complex. Al-Qaeda may remain a menace to America and its allies, yet it is hardly the only threat arrayed against the United States today—or even the most potent one. Rather, America now faces a trio of separate and distinct strategic challenges. And how it deals with them will determine its long-term success or failure in the current struggle.

AL-QAEDA "3.0"

For all intents and purposes, the organization that carried out the most devastating terrorist attack in U.S. history no longer exists. In the years since September 11, U.S. and allied counterterrorism operations have decimated the top leadership of the bin Laden network, eliminating and apprehending key operational commanders and disrupting the organization's day-to-day operations.[5] Even a partial accounting of the organization's casualties to date paints a clear picture of the successes that have been racked up by the United States and its allies.

This certainly does not mean that al-Qaeda has gone out of business, however. As the first generation of the organization's leadership has been killed or captured, a new crop of radicals has stepped in to take its place.[6] But, in the face of Coalition operations, it has also metamorphosed from a cohesive organization into a loose movement of affiliated groups, and its ideology has undergone a similar diffusion. As a result, al-Qaeda has become more an idea than an organization—a Sunni jihadist front built around a common ideology among its constituent groups, but only sporadic or ad hoc contacts between them. And its leader, Osama bin Laden, experts say, "has transitioned from being the head of a unitary terrorist organization to being the ideological leader of a 'jihadist' movement comprising many new groups that operate without direct support or direction from him or his deputy, Ayman al-Zawahiri."[7]

Iraq has served as a turning point of sorts in this evolution. Over the past two years, al-Qaeda has undeniably suffered a catastrophic reversal of fortune there. Internal communications between al-Qaeda commanders captured by Coalition forces since the start of the U.S.-led "surge" lay bare a terror movement in "extraordinary crisis," plagued by crumbling morale, a loss of local support and dramatically declining popularity.[8] It would be difficult to overstate the importance of this development. Modern-day Mesopotamia represents the cradle of the Islamic kingdom so desired by al-Qaeda and other Sunni radicals. Osama bin Laden himself has termed Baghdad to be the "capital of the caliphate," and Iraq the epicenter of the "Third World War" now raging between Islam and the West.[9] Al-Qaeda's failure there is nothing short of disastrous for the organization's ideological credibility.

But while al-Qaeda may be down, it is decidedly not out. America's early successes against the bin Laden network "have only yielded a franchised and networked enemy that is more diffuse, an ideological movement that is no longer tethered to any strict hierarchy," Defense Secretary Robert Gates warned in May 2008. "It has become an independent force of its own, capable of animating a corps of devoted followers without direct contact and capable of inspiring violence without direct orders."[10]

This network is far-flung, encompassing established affiliates in the Middle East; North Africa; and Central, South, and Southeast Asia; as well as smaller cells on virtually every continent. Yet it is also loose-knit and stateless in nature, with its various components operating independently and autonomously. Those that support them generally serve as enablers, rather than managers; they cannot hope to dictate the terms of the jihad that is being waged by these groups against the West, only to sustain it and try to mold it to suit their political purposes.

AN IRANIAN ISLAMINTERN

Unlike its Sunni counterpart, today's global Shi'a movement is based on a state-centric model, at the heart of which lies one nation: the Islamic Republic of Iran. Nearly all of the groups that make up this radical collective are tethered in some way to their chief political and ideological patron—and their threat capabilities, political stature and, in some instances, their very survival hinge directly upon Tehran's largesse.

The scope of the Islamic Republic's investment in terror is enormous. In its most recent annual report on terrorist trends, the U.S. State Department confirmed yet again that Iran remains the world's "most active state sponsor of terrorism."[11] It is a mantle that the Iranian regime has worn, and worn proudly, since the U.S. government began keeping track of terrorist trends more than a decade-and-a-half ago, animated by the ideological imperative enshrined in its constitution to "export" its revolution far beyond its borders.[12]

Iran's support of terrorism is financial; U.S. officials now say that Tehran "has a nine-digit line item in its budget for support to terrorist organizations."[13] That figure is estimated to include more than $120 million per year for its principal terrorist proxy, Hezbollah, $20 million to $30 million annually for Hamas, $2 million a year for the Palestinian Islamic Jihad, and, at least until recently, upward of $30 million a year for Iraqi insurgents.[14] It is also operational, from a deepening Iranian strategic footprint in the Palestinian Territories to the provision of arms and training to thousands of Shi'a in post-Saddam Iraq.[15] Perhaps most significant, however, is the military bulwark that the Iranian regime can offer to its terrorist affiliates against external aggression. A glimpse of this potential was on display back in 2004, when, as part of the deepening strategic ties between their two countries, Iran formally committed to defending Syria in the event of hostilities—a commitment which the Islamic Republic subsequently extended to Lebanon and Hezbollah as well.[16] Given the Islamic Republic's very public march toward "the bomb," this strategic umbrella could be nuclear in nature in the very near future, providing Iranian affiliates far greater freedom of action than ever before.

As a result of this support, Iran's various terrorist affiliates have a direct—and durable—connection to their chief sponsor. As Sheikh Naim Qassem, the deputy head of Lebanon's terrorist powerhouse, Hezbollah, told an Iranian television channel in April 2007, his organization "is committed to receiv[ing] religious instruction regarding the nature of the confrontation with Israel from al-wali al-faqih," Iranian Supreme Leader Ali Khamenei himself.[17] This direction, Qassem made clear, extends to providing sanction for the types of tactics employed by the Shi'a militia.[18] A similar connection can be seen in Iraq, where Shi'a political parties boast deep historic and ideological ties to Tehran, and Shi'a militias rely heavily on the Islamic Republic for financial aid, operational support, and political protection.

So successful has this model proven to be that it has even attracted some Sunni radicals. These "honorary Shi'a" include the anti-Israel Palestinian Islamic Jihad militia, which traces its ideology back to the teachings of the Islamic Revolution, and sees itself as "one of the many fruits on our leader Khomeini's tree."[19] More recently, it also applies to the Hamas movement, which has steadily relied on Iranian largesse since its abrupt assumption of power in the Palestinian Authority in January of 2006—and whose hostile takeover of the Gaza Strip a year later was made possible in large part through Tehran's active assistance and support.

This hub-and-spoke pattern bears little resemblance to the patch-work of dispersed Sunni jihadists now operating in the Middle East who, without explicit state linkages, are forced to scrounge for funds and weapons. Rather, the broad web of economic, political and ideo-logical bonds that Iran has managed to form with some of the world's most extreme elements is reminiscent of the model favored by the So-viet Union in its day. In a very real sense, Iran can be said to be building a latter-day, Muslim version of the Comintern assembled by the USSR during the early years of the Cold War to spread its "workers' revolu-tion" around the world.

"UNDECIDED VOTERS" IN THE MUSLIM WORLD

Islam is the world's fastest-growing religion. Its adherents already make up as much as one-fifth of humanity, and—buoyed by positive demo-graphic growth in the world's majority Muslim nations—its ranks are poised to swell in coming generations.[20] And while those who adhere to the most extreme interpretations of the religion are a distinct minority, a substantially larger percentage has proven itself sympathetic to at least certain elements of this worldview, from support for the spread of *sharia* to antipathy toward the United States.

These numbers matter a great deal. As columnist Arnaud de Borch-grave pointed out, if just one percent of the world's Muslim population embraces bin Laden's radical agenda, it would mean "12 million [or more] Muslim fanatics who believe America is the Great Satan, fount of all evil, to be attacked and demolished."[21]

If anything, de Borchgrave's estimate is exceedingly optimistic. Even those scholars who tend to downplay the prevalence of radicalism in the Muslim world concede the existence of a substantially larger problem. In their book *Who Speaks For Islam?* John Esposito and Dalia Mogahed estimate that some 7 percent of all Muslims subscribe to most—if not all—of bin Laden's extremist worldview.[22] Put another way, this means that close to a hundred million of the world's Muslims are more or less ideologically opposed to the United States and its allies. More sober assessments, meanwhile, put the number of Muslims sympathetic to at least certain parts of the radical Islamic agenda much higher: at as much as 36 percent of the world Muslim population.[23]

It should come as no surprise, then, that both strains of radical political Islam have made it their top priority to court, engage, and exploit this constituency. In a real sense, this is the center of gravity in the current conflict, and the place where our struggle against the extremist ideology of our adversaries will be won or lost.

A WIDER WAR

To their credit, U.S. officials are beginning to think bigger about the threats now arrayed against America and its allies. In his 2007 State of the Union Address, President Bush sounded a now-familiar refrain when he warned the American people about the danger they face from al-Qaeda and its ideological fellow travelers. This time, however, the commander-in-chief went further. "In recent times, it has also become clear that we face an escalating danger from Shi'ite extremists who are just as hostile to America, and are also determined to dominate the Middle East. Many are known to take direction from the regime in Iran, which is funding and arming terrorists like Hezbollah—a group second only to al-Qaeda in the American lives it has taken."[24]

To date, however, this shift is still more rhetoric than reality. Policymakers in Washington indeed have begun to show heartening signs of understanding the need for a broader definition of America's enemies. "Our strategy to combat terrorism is really only a strategy to combat Al-Qaeda," Rep. Jim Saxton, the former ranking member of the House Subcommittee on Terrorism and Unconventional Warfare, pointed out. "We are not prepared to deal—in the event hostilities occur—with terrorist organizations that are built differently."[25] But so far, U.S. strategic doctrine by and large has not adapted to account for this new set of adversaries.

This amounts to a fatal error. For the United States to forge a truly predictive and agile counterterrorism strategy, policymakers in Washington need to understand—and to exploit—the differences among its enemies. The chapters that follow offer some ideas on how they can do so, focusing on the nonmilitary areas of the current conflict, where U.S. strategy has failed to match the seriousness or the commitment demonstrated by our adversaries and has fallen short of having the scope necessary to address the complex nature of today's threat.

NOTES

1. Shaykh Usama Bin-Muhammad Bin-Laden et al., "Jihad Against Jews and Crusaders: World Islamic Front Statement," February 23, 1998.

2. An early version of this chapter appeared in the September/October 2007 issue of *The National Interest* under the title "Iran, The Rainmaker."

3. White House, Office of the Press Secretary, *National Strategy for Combating Terrorism*, September 2006, 5.

4. U.S. Department of Defense, *National Defense Strategy*, June 2008, 7-8.

5. When tallied in March 2006, more than three-quarters of al-Qaeda's pre–September 11 leadership was estimated to have been killed or captured. This list included Mohammed Atef, al-Qaeda's chief military planner, killed during a U.S. air strike near Kabul, Afghanistan in November 2001; Abu Zubaidah, a top al-Qaeda field commander, apprehended by Pakistani security forces in Faisalabad in March 2002; September 11 mastermind Khalid Sheik Mohammed, the head of al-Qaeda's global operations, similarly captured in Rawalpindi in March 2003; al-Qaeda's chief of operations for the Persian Gulf, Abu Hazim al-Shair, who was killed in a firefight with Saudi security forces in Riyadh in Mach 2004; and many others. See James Phillips, "The Evolving Al-Qaeda Threat," The Heritage Foundation *Heritage Lecture* no. 928, March 17, 2006, http://www.heritage.org/Research/HomelandSecurity/hl928.cfm.

6. Owais Tohid, "Next Wave of Al Qaeda Leadership," *Christian Science Monitor*, October 5, 2004, http://www.csmonitor.com/2004/1005/p01s04-wosc.htm.

7. William Boykin, "Al-Qaeda: Enduring Appeal," *The Journal of International Security Affairs* 15 (fall 2008): 75.

8. Martin Fletcher, "Al-Qaeda Leaders Admit: 'We Are In Crisis. There is Fear And Panic,'" *Times of London*, February 11, 2008, http://www.timesonline.co.uk/tol/news/world/iraq/article3346386.ece.

9. Osama bin Laden, Audio Message to the Muslims of Iraq in Particular and the [Islamic] Nation in General, posted on Jihadi Websites, December 28, 2004, http://www.defenddemocracy.org/publications/publications_show.htm?doc_id=512197.

10. Kristin Roberts, "Al Qaeda Now Tougher To Defeat—U.S. Defense Chief," Reuters, May 22, 2008, http://thestar.com.my/news/story.asp?file=/2008/5/22/worldupdates/2008-05-22T084500Z_01_NOOTR_RTRMDNC_0_-337036-1&sec=Worldupdates.

11. Extrapolated from "Chapter 3: State Sponsors of Terrorism Overview," in U.S. Department of State, Office of the Coordinator for Counterterrorism, *Country Reports on Terrorism 2007* (Washington, DC: U.S. Department of State, 2007), http://www.state.gov/s/ct/rls/crt/2007/103711.htm.

12. According to the country's 1979 constitution, Iran's clerical army, the *Pasdaran*, is tasked not only with the defense of the country, but with "fulfilling the ideological mission of jihad in God's way; that is, extending the sovereignty of God's law throughout the world." *Constitution of the Islamic Republic of Iran*, Preamble, October 24, 1979.

13. Under Secretary of the Treasury for Terrorism and Financial Intelligence Stuart Levey, Remarks before the 5th Annual Conference on Trade, Treasury, and Cash Management in the Middle East, Abu Dhabi, United Arab Emirates, March 7, 2007, http://uae.usembassy.gov/remarks_of_stuart_levey_.html.

14. Rachel Ehrenfeld, *Funding Evil: How Terrorism Is Financed—And How To Stop It* (Chicago: Basic Books, 2003), 125; "Hamas," Council on Foreign Relations *Backgrounder*, June 8, 2007, http://www.cfr.org/publication/8968/; Program on Humanitarian Policy and Conflict Research, Harvard University, "Palestinian Islamic Jihad of Islamic Jihad Movement in Palestine (PIJ) (Harakat al-Jihad al-Islami fi Filastin)," n.d., http://www.armed-groups.org/6/section.aspx/ViewGroup?id=69; Joshua Partlow, "U.S.: Iran, Hezbollah Training Iraqi Militants," *The Washington Post*, July 2, 2007, A08.

15. Amos Harel, "Senior IDF Officer Confirms Iran Training Militants in Gaza," *Ha'aretz* (Tel Aviv), April 22, 2007, http://www.haaretz.com/hasen /spages/851100.html; Phil Sands and Raymond Whitaker, "The Iranian Connection: From Tehran To Baghdad," *The Independent* (London), April 15, 2007, http://news.independent.co.uk/world/middle_east/article2449981.ece.

16. "Lebanese President Says Iran and Lebanon 'Strategic Allies,'" IRNA (Tehran), February 28, 2004.

17. As cited in "In An Interview Granted To An Iranian TV Channel, Sheikh Naim Qassem, Hassan Nasrallah's Deputy, Stresses That Hezbollah's Policy Of Terrorist Operations Against Israel (Including Suicide Bombings and Rocket Fire) Requires Jurisprudent Permission Of The Iranian Leadership," Intelligence and Terrorism Information Center, Israel Intelligence Heritage & Commemoration Center, April 29, 2007, http://www.terrorism-info.org .il/malam_multimedia/English/eng_n/html/hezbollah_e0407.htm.

18. Ibid.

19. Ziad Abu-Amr, *Islamic Fundamentalism in the West Bank and Gaza* (Bloomington: Indiana University Press, 1994), 101; PIJ leader Ramadan Abdallah Shallah, as cited by IRNA (Tehran), May 22, 2002.

20. Gavin W. Jones, "A Demographic Perspective On The Muslim World," *Journal of Population Research* 23, no. 2 (2006): 243–65.

21. Arnaud de Borchgrave, "Radical Islam Rising," United Press International, January 13, 2003, http://amconmag.com/2003/01_13_03/borchgrave7 .html.

22. John L. Esposito and Dalia Mogahed, *Who Speaks For Islam? What A Billion Muslims Really Think* (Washington, DC: Gallup Press, 2008).

23. Robert Satloff, "Just Like Us! Really?" *Weekly Standard* 13, no. 33 (2008), http://www.weeklystandard.com/Content/Public/Articles/000/000/015/066chpzg.asp?pg=1.

24. Ibid.

25. Jim Saxton, "Reshaping Our Iran Policy," *The National Interest* 87 (2007): 45.

2

WANTED: AN IDEOLOGICAL OFFENSIVE

During the 1930s, the bank robber Willie Sutton gained national no-toriety for a string of daring heists in New York and Philadelphia. When authorities finally caught up with "Slick Willie," as he was popularly known, he was reportedly asked about his choice of targets. His answer was simple, and iconic: "because that's where the money is."

The United States could learn a thing or two from Willie Sutton. Today, Washington may be dominating the various military battlefields of the Long War. But it is increasingly clear that the decisive arena of our current struggle against the forces of radical Islam is ideological, rather than military.

Our adversaries understand this very well. As long ago as 2002, Osama bin Laden had already identified the "media war" as one of the "strongest methods" for promoting al-Qaeda's objectives.[1] He directed his organization to establish an information committee "charged with spreading the Al-Qa'ida vision of jihad to all Muslims."[2] More than half a decade later, this effort has become a multinational multimedia conglomerate, complete with a dedicated production arm known as *As-Sahab*, a mouthpiece for training and operations (the Global Islamic Media Front), and a network of fifty or more websites, the objectives of which range from providing information to *jihadis* in the field to disseminating propaganda on forums frequented by sympathizers.[3] All of this is underpinned by a complex seven-pronged strategy that promotes psychological warfare; publicity and propaganda; data mining;

recruitment and mobilization; networking; information sharing; and operational planning and coordination.[4]

"The sophistication of this communications strategy is stunning," Lieutenant General William Boykin, the Bush administration's former point man on al-Qaeda, wrote. "Bin Laden has been quick to leverage every misstep by the West for propaganda purposes, and to seize every opportunity to bolster the morale of his followers and recruit new cells and 'holy warriors.'"[5]

Nor is al-Qaeda the only one. The Islamic Republic of Iran has similarly marshaled massive resources in support of the "exportation" of its radical revolutionary strain of Shi'a Islam. Its state-run Islamic Republic of Iran Broadcasting (IRIB) media network alone boasts a budget of some eight hundred million dollars annually, and operates nine national radio stations, as well as twenty-six local and eight national TV stations—including three satellite channels.[6] Of these, the most high-profile is Press TV, a twenty-four-hour English-language satellite television channel launched with great fanfare in the summer of 2007 as part of the Iranian regime's effort to "break the global stranglehold" of Western media on world public opinion.[7]

Further afield, Iran has also bankrolled the flagship political warfare arm of its chief terrorist proxy, Hezbollah. Since its establishment in a conservative suburb of Beirut in June 1991, *al-Manar* (Arabic for "the beacon") has become a broadcasting powerhouse. It boasts multiple satellite feeds, correspondents in more than fifteen countries, a dynamic website, and continuous multilingual coverage of global events.[8] Through its operations, Hezbollah's media mouthpiece has helped to transform how terrorists, insurgents, and radicals of various political stripes communicate their messages to the outside world.

Both efforts have been aided by the media revolution that has swept over the Middle East over the past two decades. Once an informational backwater, where residents relied almost exclusively on Western or stagnant state media for their daily news and information, the region has experienced an explosion of digital news outlets in recent years.

The current Arab media age has emerged in essentially two waves. The first of these took place during the late 1970s and early 1980s. That time period saw the rise of influential "pan-Arab" print media, embodied by such publications as London's prominent, Saudi-financed *Al-Sharq al-Awsat* newspaper and its later competitor, *Al-Hayat*. These newspapers—as well as a host of smaller ones—positioned themselves as more authentic antidotes to Western news sources.[9] The second, more transformative, epoch began in the latter part of the 1990s, with the simultaneous advent of Arab satellite television and the proliferation of the Internet.

The numbers tell the story. In 1998, there were just four digital television platforms in the Middle East; today, there are at least 280 Arab satellite television channels.[10] Of these, without a doubt the most famous is *al-Jazeera*. The Dubai-based satellite television channel, the brainchild of Qatari emir Sheikh Hamad Khalifa al-Thani, was barely a blip on the media radar when it began operations in 1996. Since September 11, however, it has rocketed to international prominence, now serving as a primary source of news to an estimated audience of some sixty to seventy million regular viewers worldwide. And increasingly, it is not the only one. Over the past several years, a number of other Arab satellite broadcasters, such as Dubai's *al-Arabiya* and multiple foreign media operations (like Russia's *Rusiya Al-Yaum* or America's *Alhurra*) have gotten into the Middle East television game.

Internet usage has experienced a similar surge. Between 2000 and 2007, regional access grew by an astounding 920 percent, and now stands at 33.5 million users.[11] In comparative terms, the Middle East still trails other regions; just 17.4 percent of the region's inhabitants currently have access to the World Wide Web (as compared to 71.1 percent of those in North America and 43.4 percent of those in Europe).[12] But it represents an increasingly powerful and transformative medium of regional communications.

In this changing informational landscape, our opponents have done more than simply survived. They have thrived, leveraging new modes of communications and multispectrum media to amplify their message.

What can the United States do to counter this outreach? Until now, policymakers in Washington have not bothered to find out. With very few exceptions, they have neglected to identify themes and messages that could discredit al-Qaeda's ideology, or ways of diminishing the legitimacy of the Islamic Republic of Iran at home and abroad. They will need to do so if they hope to mount a serious ideological offensive in the "battle for hearts and minds" now underway in the wider Muslim world.

DISCREDITING AL-QAEDA'S MESSAGE

"When people see a strong horse and a weak horse, by nature they will like the strong horse," Osama bin Laden declared proudly in the wake of the September 11 attacks.[13] At the time, the terror leader's triumphalism appeared to be warranted. His organization had just leapt onto the world stage by carrying out the most devastating terrorist attacks in America's history. Its cadres appeared to be on the march. And, inspired by the example of the Soviet Union's retreat from Afghanistan more than a decade earlier, its leadership thought it could do much more.

Today, however, the situation is very different. In the nearly eight years since September 11, al-Qaeda's radical, exclusionary worldview; its brutal, indiscriminate tactics; and its lack of a positive political agenda have progressively turned away potential recruits and alienated sympathizers across the Muslim world.

This has been confirmed by recent studies that suggest international support for the radical ideology embodied by al-Qaeda has declined precipitously. As the prestigious Pew Center noted, backing for bin Laden dropped dramatically in a number of key nations between 2003 and 2007, falling from 56 to 20 percent in Jordan; from 20 to just 1 percent in Lebanon, and; from 59 to 41 percent in Indonesia.[14] Even in Saudi Arabia, home to fifteen of the nineteen September 11 hijackers, bin Laden and his followers have become increasingly unpopular: according to a 2007 survey conducted by the polling group Terror Free Tomorrow, nearly two-thirds of Saudis hold an unfavorable view of bin Laden and al-Qaeda, and 61 percent place defeating al-Qaeda and other *jihadi* groups at the top of the list of their government's priorities.[15]

By all accounts, this alienation is taking place on an intellectual level as well. A number of prominent Islamic thinkers have progressively drifted away from al-Qaeda's uncompromising worldview. Perhaps the most notorious of these is Sayyid Imam al-Sharif, better known as "Dr. Fadl," an Egyptian Islamist who served as a key figure in the original al-Qaeda and a mentor to the organization's ideologue and second-in-command, Ayman al-Zawahiri. "Dr. Fadl," now languishing in an Egyptian prison, appears to have had a change of heart, penning a new book in which he rejects "aggression" and violence against the enemies of Islam.[16] Other Islamist notables have followed suit. Saudi scholar

Salman al-Oudah, one of Osama bin Laden's key intellectual influences, has taken the unprecedented step of publicly chastising the al-Qaeda leader about his excesses. In a September 2007 television interview, al-Oudah beseeched bin Laden:

> My brother Osama, how much blood has been spilt? How many innocent people, children, elderly, and women have been killed . . . in the name of al-Qa'ida? Will you be happy to meet God Almighty carrying the burden of these hundreds of thousands or millions [of victims] on your back?[17]

India's influential Deobandi Islamic movement, the progenitor of much of today's radical Islamic thought in South Asia, appears to have made a similar about-face. In May 2008, the group issued a new fatwa condemning terrorism and promoting sectarian reconciliation. "Those who use the Koran and the teachings of the Prophet Muhammad to justify terror are merely upholding a lie," the message said.[18]

Terrorism experts have taken note of this trend. Peter Bergen of the New America Foundation, one of the Western scholars best acquainted with bin Laden, has identified four "long term strategic weaknesses" that cumulatively could serve as the harbinger of al-Qaeda's destruction.[19] The first derives from the organization's penchant for targeting its co-religionists. "Al Qaeda and its affiliates have killed thousands of Muslim civilians . . . since September 11," including in Afghanistan, Jordan, and of course Iraq, Bergen and his colleague Paul Cruickshank of New York University point out.[20] This has contributed to declining popularity for the movement as a whole, and growing alienation from even those Muslims who were once sympathetic to the organization's goals.

The second is al-Qaeda's lack of a positive vision for the future. "We know what they're against, but what are they really for?" Bergen points out, noting that, beyond the general goal of restoring the caliphate, neither Osama bin Laden nor his emissaries have articulated anything resembling a positive agenda for Muslim empowerment or prosperity. Instead, potential supporters are faced with the prospect of "Taliban-style regimes from Morocco to Indonesia."[21]

The third chink in al-Qaeda's ideological armor lies in its insurmountable list of adversaries. Al-Qaeda has identified practically every government, organization, religion, and ethnic group as its enemy. From Muslims who don't happen to share the movement's radical worldview; to corrupt, Westernized governments; to international institutions that are seen as lackeys of the Zionist-Crusader alliance, none have been spared the organization's wrath. And if no one is with al-Qaeda, it means that everyone is against it.

Finally, and perhaps most fundamentally, the bin Laden network has failed to engage in modern politics. Indeed, al-Qaeda's radical, exclusionary ideology—rooted in the Wahhabi/Salafi strain of radical political Islam—is irreconcilably opposed to either Western values or participation in modern politics. All of which "prevents them from making the real-world compromises that would allow them to engage in genuine politics," Bergen and Cruickshank point out.[22] That means that the bin Laden network is destined to remain on the margins of world politics, more often than not being driven by current events rather than shaping them.

Washington, however, so far has failed to capitalize upon this trend. It has neglected to highlight the cost that al-Qaeda's murderous ideology has imposed on the Islamic world, where the organization's tactics and methods have claimed exponentially more victims than in the West. It likewise has done little to underscore the bin Laden network's fundamental lack of a positive political vision, or the organization's profound failure—in Iraq and elsewhere—to better the lives of its purported constituents. Nor has it done enough to emphasize that al-Qaeda's avowed goal of a global caliphate and the destruction of all unbelievers is, for all intents and purposes, hopeless.

This state of affairs is both surprising and disheartening, since the totalitarian worldview espoused by our enemies is so distinctly unappealing, even to Muslims. "Osama Bin Laden may be admired in some quarters for his willingness to stand up to the United States," terrorism scholar James S. Robbins points out, "but few fully endorse his ideological beliefs."[23] Fewer still have any interest in living in the type of society preferred by bin Laden and his ilk—one in which individual choice is shunned in favor of religiously imposed consensus, and personal freedoms are subjugated to the harshest possible interpretation of *sharia* law.

The task of American strategy, then, must be to bring these deficiencies to the fore. U.S. political outreach to the Muslim world should focus in part on discrediting the radical, intolerant ideology of al-Qaeda and its affiliates, debunking their contentions about the West, and delegitimizing their authority to speak on behalf of all Muslims.

PRESENTING AN IDEOLOGICAL CHALLENGE TO IRAN

If diminishing al-Qaeda's global appeal lies in discrediting its message and ideology to the wider Muslim world, the key to diluting Iran's ideological power lies within the Islamic Republic itself, along the fault line between the ruling regime and its captive population.

This is because Iran is a country in the throes of a profound demographic transformation. Its population of 70 million is overwhelmingly young; nearly half (48.8 percent) is aged twenty-four or younger, according to official regime statistics.[24] Iran's ruling elite, by contrast, is aging and infirm. Thirty years after coming to power, the majority of the Islamic Republic's original revolutionaries are in their late sixties and early seventies, and many are said to be ailing.[25]

This generational divide is significant. It suggests that more than half of all Iranians have little or no memory of the Islamic Revolution itself. And while a minority of them do identify with its foundational principles, the majority give clear signs of being increasingly discontented with their country's economic and political conditions. In its 2008 opinion survey of Iranian attitudes, for example, the Foundation for the Promotion of Democracy in Iran found that nearly 60 percent of all respondents believed Iran to be headed in the "wrong direction."[26] Similarly, 61 percent of the one thousand Iranians surveyed as part of Terror Free Tomorrow's 2007 nationwide survey of opinion within the Islamic Republic opposed the "unelected rule of Supreme Leader" Ali Khamenei, and nearly 80 percent expressed support for a system of government "where all leaders are elected."[27]

To date, however, the United States has done precious little to harness this potential. Rather, it has consistently neglected opportunities to engage the Iranian people at the expense of its regime.

The most obvious is economic. In the early days of the Islamic Republic, when the initial euphoria of their revolution began to be replaced by more mundane concerns among Iran's new rulers, an aide is said to have asked Supreme Leader Ruhollah Khomeini about his plan to combat the creeping inflation then beginning to plague the country. Khomeini, the story goes, brushed aside these concerns, responding disdainfully that the Islamic Revolution "was not about the price of watermelons."[28] The message was crystal clear: to Iran's ayatollahs, politics mattered more than affluence.

Fast forward three decades, and the situation remains very much the same. Iran's rulers may pay lip service to widening domestic prosperity. During his successful 2005 presidential campaign, Mahmoud Ahmadinejad even ran a populist campaign focused on combating corruption, famously promising the Persian equivalent of "a chicken in every pot." In practice, however, there's no shortage of signs that the Islamic Republic has fundamentally failed its people on an economic level.

Today, Iran is in the doldrums, buffeted by the global economic crisis and burdened by unsustainable federal spending. Inflation now officially stands at some 30 percent, while the costs of staple goods continue to rise—outpacing the ability of ordinary Iranians to pay for them.[29] Unemployment is rampant, officially pegged at over 10 percent but unofficially estimated to be as much as 25 percent.[30] This has been compounded by widespread and severe underemployment in various sectors, caused by a chronic shortage of viable job opportunities—and an acute failure on the part of the Iranian government to create more.

Related social indicators present an equally bleak picture. According to statistics compiled by the United Nations, nearly a quarter of the Iranian population now lives under the poverty line.[31] Prostitution is similarly out of control; although official statistics are hard to come by, unofficial estimates put the number of sex workers in the Islamic Republic at several hundred thousand.[32] Over the past several years, inability to keep pace with this skyrocketing trend has led Iranian authorities to contemplate a range of remedial measures, from "temporary marriages" to sanctioned brothels known as "chastity houses."[33] Drug addiction is also rampant, fueled by the widespread opium trade taking place in neighboring Afghanistan; in 2005, the United Nations estimated Iran to have the highest rate of addiction in the world, with nearly 3 percent of the country's population addicted to opiates.[34]

America has the ability to harness this malaise to dilute the power of the Iranian regime. By drawing greater attention to the deformities of their current government, and to the abject failure of Khomeini's brand of radical political Islam as a governing ideology, the United States can tap into the groundswell of domestic discontent now visible in Iran's markets, on its street corners, and within its university campuses.

It certainly has the political credibility to do so. In no small measure because of its lack of official engagement with Tehran over the past three decades, Washington is seen on the Iranian street as an "honest broker," and as a potential ally of those Iranians seeking fundamental political change. It is no wonder that some have described Iran as "the ultimate red state"[35]—a nation in which resistance to an entrenched, thuggish theocracy has cultivated natural allies for the West in its struggle with radical Islam.

The United States can leverage this credibility to engage the Iranian public directly on at least two topics. The first is the Iranian regime's quest for a nuclear capability. For years, conventional wisdom has held that "going nuclear" is one of a handful of issues upon which both the Iranian leadership and its people agree. The reality, however, is more complex. By all accounts, the quest for nuclear *power* is a widely popular effort within Iran—one that is supported by a majority of the country's population on cultural, historical, or political grounds. Indeed, an early 2008 poll carried out by the polling group worldpublicopinion.org found that fully 81 percent of the seven hundred Iranians surveyed believed it was "very important" for their country to master nuclear technology.[36] But that is where the consensus ends. In the same survey, nearly 60 percent of respondents said they were opposed to the development of nuclear *weapons*, terming them to be "against the teachings of Islam."[37] Many others, Iran watchers say, are "concerned, ambivalent or simply uninformed" about their government's atomic intentions.[38]

Washington has not yet exploited these fissures. Since the start of the international crisis over the Islamic Republic's nuclear ambitions some seven years ago, the United States has consistently failed to clearly and unambiguously communicate to the Iranian people its support for their right to nuclear power, as well as its misgivings over what their regime plans to do with it. And because it has not, the Iranian leadership has managed to successfully monopolize the national dialogue over its nuclear ambitions. By doing so, it has managed to parlay what is essentially an insular regime priority into a point of national pride.

This constitutes a critical error. If fully mobilized against their regime's nuclear effort, the Iranian people have the power to serve as one of the West's most potent weapons in opposing an atomic Iran. In order for that to happen, however, they will need to hear, clearly and unequivocally, that their government's atomic enterprise carries with it potentially catastrophic costs for them, ranging from economic isolation to all-out war.

Another revolves around the Iranian regime's prominent role in international terrorism. Over the years, the Iranian leadership has provided aid and comfort to a bevy of international radicals, often at the expense of ordinary Iranians. This disconnect has engendered a great deal of domestic resentment. In the wake of Hezbollah's summer 2006 war with Israel, for example, Iran's extensive financial support for Lebanon's Shi'ites became a serious bone of domestic contention, with ordinary Iranians publicly questioning—and condemning—their government's skewed strategic priorities.[39] This very public expression of resentment provides an important glimpse into the ideological gulf that exists between the Iran's government and its people. Many Iranians feel neglected and abandoned by their regime, which appears more concerned with the imperative of "exporting the revolution" than providing for the security and prosperity of its own citizens.

The West is in a position to amplify this perception. By highlighting the Iranian regime's extensive support for radicalism abroad—and its concurrent failure to deliver concrete economic and political dividends at home—the United States and its allies can help further diminish the political legitimacy and authority of the regime in Tehran.

Finally, the United States has the power to support both ideological and religious alternatives to the current regime in Tehran. In his seminal 1951 book, *The True Believer*, American philosopher Eric Hoffer famously noted that ideological mass movements are inherently competitive by nature.[40] They draw their adherents from the same groups of people, and hold the same appeal of a different political order. Therefore, Hoffer postulated, "The problem of stopping a mass movement is often a matter of substituting one movement for another."[41]

The current Iranian leadership understands this very well. Since they came to power three decades ago, Iran's religious revolutionaries have waged a dogged and determined ideological war against Persian culture and Persian nationalism. They have repeatedly attempted to marginalize Persian holidays in favor of those that extol Shi'a Islam.[42] For years, they maintained a ban on naming Iranian children with pre-Islamic names, such as Darius and Cyrus.[43] They have even attempted to destroy what is perhaps the greatest symbol of Iran's cultural heritage, the tomb of the great Zoroastrian King Cyrus, who lived from 576 to 530 BCE.[44]

These efforts are logical. Iran is an ancient and proud civilization, with a history stretching back thousands of years. The Islamic Republic, meanwhile, is just three decades old, an ideological "Johnny-come-lately" which has imposed a perversion of religious doctrine upon its own people (discussed in greater detail below). Its leaders are thus deeply aware of, and antagonistic to, any manifestations of pre-Islamic culture with the power to challenge their monopoly on legitimacy.

Many such examples exist. Among the most famous is the legend of Kaveh the Blacksmith, a story narrated by the venerated Persian poet Abolqasem Ferdowsi in his tenth-century volume *Shahnameh* (Epic of Kings). Kaveh, the legend goes, was a blacksmith who toiled under the yoke of the tyrant Zahak, whose pact with the devil had made him a "dragon king" who demanded human sacrifice to ease his insatiable hunger. After losing eighteen of his sons in this manner, Kaveh led a successful popular revolt to unseat Zahak, using as his standard his blacksmith's apron, which came to be known as the Derafsh Kaviani, or "Flag of Kaveh."[45]

When first told, this myth was a thinly veiled euphemism for Persian resistance to Muslim conquest during the Middle Ages. But its narrative of independence, freedom, and opposition to unjust rule continues to resonate today, and the myth of Kaveh remains readily recognizable to most Iranians, irrespective of ethnicity.

By hoisting the Derafsh Kaviani—through harnessing this and other compelling national narratives—the United States has the power to present (and expand) a serious ideological challenge to the regime in Tehran. Just as important, it can provide much-needed confirmation to ordinary Iranians that it understands their culture and supports their urge for freedom in a way that their government does not—indeed, cannot. And therein lies the key to further weakening the ideological bonds that connect the Iranian people to the regime that rules over them.

Nationalist narratives are not the only ones with the power to challenge the Islamic Republic's legitimacy. The creation of the Islamic Republic in 1979 marked a dramatic departure from centuries of established religious tradition. Before the Ayatollah Ruhollah Khomeini's assumption of power in Tehran, and his subsequent establishment of the *velayat-e faqih* (Guardianship of the Jurisprudent) as the governing ideology of his new Islamic Republic, Shi'a Muslims had hewed to a "quietist" tradition, eschewing participation in contemporary politics in favor of private and communal asceticism. The reasons were logical; at just 15 percent of the Islamic world, Shi'a were a distinct minority, and they were often persecuted by their co-religionists for their failure to adhere to the dominant Sunni interpretation of the faith. Upon coming to power in Tehran, however, Khomeini flipped this historical formula on its head, articulating a new concept of theocratic Islamic rule and religiously motivated foreign interventionism. The goal was outlined in his manifesto, *Islamic Government*, published on the eve of Iran's 1979 revolution: to "fight the rule of the false God" and displace non-Islamic regimes "so that a stable and legitimate Islamic [world] government may be established gradually."[46]

For the following decade, Khomeini's religious clout kept criticism of the *velayat-e faqih* at bay, even as his political cunning allowed him to eliminate competitors to his religious and ideological agenda. Khomeini's death in 1989, however, created a tremendous political crisis in Tehran, as the Ayatollah's acolytes searched for a suitable successor to consolidate power within the Islamic Republic. None were readily apparent; Khomeini's religious authority and his unique position as the progenitor of the Islamic Republic made it impossible to choose an equally qualified and charismatic successor dedicated to preserving his legacy. Iran's clerical elite was forced to make do, and it quickly closed ranks behind a relatively junior cleric named Ali Khamenei, appointing him to the post of *vali-e faqih*, or Supreme Leader. The move caused serious dissent among many of Iran's religious leaders, who questioned Khamenei. After all, as Iran scholar Mehdi Khalaji has put it, "Khamenei was a *hojatolislam* [junior cleric, literally a "proof of Islam"] in the morning, and the Supreme Leader in the afternoon."[47] He was, in other words, perceived by many to be a pretender to Khomeini's throne.

The situation remains very much the same today. Khamenei may still be Iran's Supreme Leader, with ultimate authority over the country's domestic and foreign policy, as well as its overall ideological line. But his religious role as *marja taqlid*, or model of religious emulation, for all Iranians—let alone all Shi'a—is far from absolute or unchallenged. As scholars such as Vali Nasr have noted, there are currently a number of clerics who command far greater religious legitimacy among the Shi'a faithful, inside and outside Iran.[48]

The most senior of these Grand Ayatollahs is Ali Sistani, Iraq's most powerful religious figure. Since the U.S. invasion of Iraq in 2003, Sistani has emerged as a key power broker in the shifting alliances and political jockeying taking place on the territory of the former Ba'athist state. He has played a mostly constructive role in that capacity, advocating restraint from his religious followers in their dealings with the Coalition, and preserving their religious and political independence despite massive pressure from Tehran. Indeed, so great is Sistani's religious authority among Shi'a Muslims that his support was instrumental to the success of the United States–led "surge" in 2007–2008, and a key factor in the ultimate ratification of the status of forces agreement signed between the United States and Iraq in late 2008.[49]

Sistani's preeminent status makes him a de facto ideological competitor of sorts to Iran's current Supreme Leader, and the Iranian leadership has responded accordingly. Since the start of the Iraq war in 2003, Iranian authorities have alternately cajoled, bribed, and threatened the Iraqi cleric into accepting their religious primacy, but to no avail. Tehran's trepidation, in this regard, is Washington's opportunity. By amplifying Sistani's message about the need for regional coexistence, and by contrasting it with Iran's calls for a civilizational war against the West, the U.S. can help frame the Iraqi cleric as the true voice of Shi'a religious doctrine, and dilute the Islamic Republic's status as the standard-bearer of religious politics in the Shi'a world.

LEARNING FROM OTHERS

All too often, when it comes to framing the current conflict, the United States tends to forget that it is not alone. The magnitude of the terrorist attacks of September 11 have spawned a sort of American exceptionalism, in which the United States believes that it holds the premium on both an understanding of the ideology of our adversaries, and the proper responses to it. Nothing could be further from the truth. Many countries around the world are currently engaged in a similar struggle against the forces of radical Islam, and the United States can learn a great deal from their successes and failures in the struggle for Muslim "hearts and minds."

Central Asia is a case in point. Between them, the region's five former Soviet republics—Kazakhstan, Kyrgyzstan, Uzbekistan, Tajikistan, and Turkmenistan—are home to some 47 million Muslims. Islam has a long and storied history there, having been introduced by invading Arabs in the late seventh century. But the religious tradition in the region has always been pluralistic, and peaceful. And for much of the twentieth century, it was practiced informally and privately—a casualty of the Soviet Union's official ban on organized religion.

As a result, and in contrast to their co-religionists in the Middle East, Central Asia's Muslims have not yet been inculcated with the radical, uncompromising brand of political Islam actively exported by

Saudi Arabia for much of the past half-century. Rather, they are still ideological newborns who are only now beginning to define themselves in relation to the modern Muslim world and its prevailing ideological currents.

Local governments understand this well, and have made the "inoculation" of their populations against Islamist ideology a cardinal priority. "Central Asian governments, especially those in Uzbekistan and Kyrgyzstan, have developed an educational system—from kindergarten through the university level—that inculcates the moral norms and social principles of tolerant Islam, and that respects the value of any human life (Muslim, Christian, Jewish, or other)," writes scholar Evgueni Novikov. This system is extensive:

> [It] provides textbooks for schools, cartoons for children, education for imams of local mosques, a network of counselors in Islamic affairs for central and local administrations, and television and radio talk shows that challenge the Wahhabi interpretation of the *Koran* and *Hadith* and provide listeners with an alternative, moderate, religious vision. Similarly, these governments have created a network of educational establishments and research centers that champion the tolerant and peaceful ideas of Islam and condemn Wahhabi ideas. Students of madrassas and universities in Tashkent and Bishkek study Arabic intensively, and upon graduation not only can read and interpret the *Koran* and *Hadith*, but also teach in Arabic. Graduates of these educational establishments become knowledgeable imams for mosques and theology teachers for public schools.[50]

Washington has been slow to take advantage of the Central Asian experience, however. In recent years, the U.S. government has focused overwhelmingly on the deficiencies of local governments in the political and human rights arenas, rather than on their potential benefit to the ideological war effort. Ongoing worries over political repression and authoritarian practices by the governments in question have prevented the United States from meaningfully engaging with them in the "war of ideas," or from harnessing their tangible contributions to this struggle (from the creation of moderate primary school textbooks to the cultivation of a new generation of Islamic scholars that has proven itself largely immune to Wahhabism's allure).

This constitutes a major error. As Novikov notes, "official Washington understandably does not wish to condone or ignore the draconian police measures employed by some of its Coalition partners—measures that often violate individual rights and liberties. Neither, however, should it wish to undermine these governments in their struggle against radical Islam, which is even less likely to adhere to Western values."[51] Instead, America's approach to the region, and to the regimes that populate it, should reflect an understanding that Central Asia numbers among the next great battlefields in the struggle against radical Islam—one of very few places in the world with the potential to turn the tide of the conflict decisively in our favor, or against it.

Africa is another. Islam is now the second largest religion on the African continent, followed by some 45 percent of its roughly 137 million inhabitants. And while traditional interpretations of the religion have been more or less moderate, radical Islam has increasingly made inroads throughout the continent in recent years, as manifested by the introduction of *sharia* law in parts of Nigeria and Somalia's short, ill-fated experiment with Islamist rule.[52]

The reasons for this radicalization are manifold. The poverty endemic throughout Africa's various regions has made its constituencies susceptible to religious radicalization. So has the pull of traditional centers of Islamic learning, such as Egypt and Saudi Arabia, and the active proselytization of various Islamic charities, which have made the continent a major priority. It is no wonder that the al-Qaeda network has found fertile soil in places like Morocco, Algeria, and Somalia, where the bin Laden network has succeeded in co-opting local Islamists and establishing a substantial beachhead.[53]

These inroads have not gone unchallenged, however. Scattered throughout the continent are competing interpretations of Islam, and challengers willing to offer different perspectives on piety, the role of religion and politics, and the juxtaposition of Islam and Western values.

Of these, Hassan al-Turabi is among the most prominent. A hard-line Islamist cleric, Turabi served as the chief ideologue of Sudan's brutal National Islamic Front from the time it seized power in 1989 to its political fragmentation a decade later. In that capacity, he was the Khartoum regime's ideological point of contact with all manner of Islamic radicals, from al-Qaeda to Hezbollah. Today, however, Turabi plays a very different role. Since falling out with his one-time compatriot, Sudanese president Omar el-Bashir, in the late 1990s, Turabi has emerged as a leading opposition figure in that country. He now heads Sudan's opposition Popular Congress Party, and advocates a more enlightened religious conservatism—one that rejects the forcible imposition of *sharia* law on non-Muslims,[54] advocates the empowerment of women,[55] and promotes limits on the power of governments to interfere in the personal lives of individuals.[56]

Is this volte-face genuine, or simply the product of political expediency? Only time will tell. For the moment, however, the political and religious ideas advocated by Turabi appear to be at odds with those of his one-time "hero," Osama bin Laden. As such, they—and others like them—can help amplify America's message to the Muslim world about the bankruptcy of al-Qaeda's worldview.

As the foregoing discussion suggests, the ideological authority of al-Qaeda is far from absolute. It is vulnerable to properly calibrated messages that highlight the poverty of its ideas, the costs of its ideological program, and the dire consequences should it succeed in its radical endeavor. The Iranian regime is similarly bankrupt, on both an ideological and a practical level. The task of U.S. strategic outreach in the years ahead should be to exploit these strategies as part of a coherent ideological offensive.

NOTES

1. "Letter to Mullah Mohammed 'Omar from Osama bin Laden," as catalogued in *Harmony and Disharmony: Exploiting Al-Qa'ida's Organizational Vulnerabilities* (New York: West Point Combating Terrorism Center, February 2006), http://ctc.usma.edu/aq/pdf/AFGP-2002-600321-Trans.pdf.

2. "None Assigned (Al-Qa'ida Goals and Structure)," as catalogued in *Harmony and Disharmony: Exploiting Al-Qa'ida's Organizational Vulnerabilities* (New York: West Point Combating Terrorism Center, February 2006), http://ctc.usma.edu/aq/aq_000078.asp.

3. Shaun Waterman, "Analysis: Al-Qaeda's Production Unit," United Press International, September 20, 2007, http://www.upi.com/Emerging _Threats/2007/09/20/Analysis_Al-Qaidas_video_production_unit/UPI-10601190302473/2; Marc Lynch, "Al Qaeda's Media Strategy," *The National Interest* no. 83 (2006): 50–56; Gabriel Weimann, *Terror on the Internet: The New Arena, the New Challenges* (Washington, DC: United States Institute of Peace Press, 2006), 15, 67.

4. Abdul Hameed Bakier, "Islamist Websites Succeed in Recruiting Muslims for Jihad," Jamestown Foundation *Terrorism Focus* 3, no. 46 (2006), http://www.jamestown.org/single/?no_cache=1&tx_ttnews[tt_news]=983; Michael

Scheuer, "Al-Qaeda's Media Doctrine: Evolution from Cheerleader to Opinion Shaper," Jamestown Foundation *Terrorism Focus* 4, no. 15 (2007), http://www.jamestown.org/single/?no_cache=1&tx_ttnews[tt_news]=4177; Lynch, "Al Qaeda's Media Strategy"; Habib Trabelsi, "Al-Qaeda Takes Jihad to Media Four Years after 9/11," *Middle East Online*, September 9, 2005, http://www.middle-east-online.com/english/features/?id=14500; Gabriel Weimann, "Terrorists and their Tools—Part II," *YaleGlobal*, April 26, 2004, http://yaleglobal.yale.edu/display.article?id=3768.

5. William Boykin, "Al-Qaeda: Enduring Appeal," *The Journal of International Security Affairs* 15 (2008): 76.

6. "Country Profile: Iran," BBC (London), November 21, 2008, http://news.bbc.co.uk/2/hi/middle_east/country_profiles/790877.stm#media; Avi Jorisch and Salameh Nematt, "Inside Hizballah's Al-Manar Television," Washington Institute for Near East Policy *Policywatch* 917, November 18, 2007, http://www.washingtoninstitute.org/templateC05.php?CID=2188; "Press TV's Budget Is 25 Billion Toomans," Mehr (Tehran), July 30, 2007, http://www.mehrnews.com/fa/NewsDetail.aspx?NewsID=519985; Jamal Dajani, "The Arab Media Revolution," *PBS Frontline*, March 27, 2007, http://www.pbs.org/frontlineworld/stories/newswar/war_arabmedia.html; Philip Fiske de Gouveia, "Iran's Media Battleground," *Guardian* (London), February 21, 2006, http://www.guardian.co.uk/international/story/0,,1714077,00.html; Sebastian Usher, "Iran's Leaders Harness Media Power," BBC (London), March 14, 2006, http://news.bbc.co.uk/2/hi/middle_east/4804328.stm; Transatlantic Institute, *Monitoring Arab TV In Europe: Al Jazeera, Iqra And Al Alam*, February 1–15, 2005, http://www.transatlanticinstitute.org/medias/publications/179.pdf; Ramin Karimian and Sha'banali Bahrampour, "Pushing the Limits: Iran's Islamic Revolution at Twenty," *Middle East Report* 212 (1999): 38–39.

7. "Iran Launches Its Answer to CNN, BBC World," Fars (Tehran), June 24, 2007, http://english.farsnews.com/newstext.php?nn=8604030340.

8. Avi Jorisch, *Beacon of Hatred: Inside Hizballah's Al-Manar Television* (Washington, DC: Washington Institute for Near East Policy, 2004), 20.

9. See Jon B. Alterman, *New Media, New Politics? From Satellite Television to the Internet in the Arab World* (Washington, DC: Washington Institute for Near East Policy, 1998), 5–14; See also S. Abdullah Schleifer, "Media Explosion in the Arab World: The Pan-Arab Satellite Broadcasters," *Transnational Broadcasting Studies Journal* 1 (1998), http://www.tbsjournal.com/Archives/Fall98/Articles1/Pan-Arab_bcasters/pan-arab_bcasters.html.

10. Chris Forrester, "Digital Platforms in the Middle East," *Transnational Broadcasting Studies Journal* 1 (1998), http://www.tbsjournal.com/Archives/Fall98/Articles1/Digital_platforms/digital_platforms.html; Alan L. Heil Jr., "Rate of Arabic Language TV Start-Ups Shows No Sign of Abating," *Arab Media & Society* 2 (2007), http://www.arabmediasociety.com/?article=180.

11. "Internet Users in the Middle East," internetworldstats.com, December 2007, http://www.internetworldstats.com/stats5.htm.

12. "World Internet Users," internetworldstats.com, December 2007, http://www.internetworldstats.com/stats.htm.

13. As cited in James Poniewozik, "The Banality of Bin Laden," *Time*, December 13, 2001, http://www.time.com/time/nation/article/0,8599,188329,00.html.

14. Pew Global Attitudes Project, "Global Unease with Major World Powers," June 27, 2007, http://pewglobal.org/reports/pdf/256.pdf.

15. Terror Free Tomorrow, "Saudi Arabians Overwhelmingly Reject Bin Laden, Al Qaeda, Saudi Fighters in Iraq, and Terrorism; Also Among Most Pro-American in Muslim World," January 2008, http://www.terrorfreetomorrow.org/upimagestft/TFT%20Saudi%20Arabia%20Survey.pdf.

16. Lawrence Wright, "The Rebellion Within," *The New Yorker*, June 2, 2008, http://www.newyorker.com/reporting/2008/06/02/080602fa_fact_wright.

17. As cited in Peter Bergen and Paul Cruickshank, "Special Report: Is Al Qa'ida in Pieces?" *Independent* (London), June 22, 2008, http://www.independent.co.uk/news/world/asia/special-report-is-al-qaida-in-p.htmls-850606.html.

18. As cited in Britta Sandberg, "Turning Their Backs on Jihad," *Spiegel* (Hamburg), July 14, 2008, http://www.spiegel.de/international/world/0,1518,565750,00.html.

19. Peter Bergen, Testimony before the U.S. House of Representatives Committee on Homeland Security's Subcommittee on Intelligence, Information Sharing and Terrorism Risk Assessment, July 30, 2008, http://www.newamerica.net/publications/resources/2008/reassessing_threat_future_al_qa_ida_and_its_implications_homeland_security.

20. Peter Bergen and Paul Cruickshank, "The Unraveling," *The New Republic*, June 11, 2008, http://www.tnr.com/story_print.html?id=702bf6d5-a37a-4e3e-a491-fd72bf6a9da1.

21. Ibid.

22. Ibid.

23. James S. Robbins, "Al-Qaeda Versus Democracy," *The Journal of International Security Affairs* 9 (2005): 57.

24. Statistical Centre of Iran, Vice-Presidency for Strategic Planning and Supervision, Islamic Republic of Iran, n.d., http://www.sci.org.ir/portal/faces/public/sci_en/sci_en.Glance/sci_en.pop.

25. For example, persistent rumors have declared Iranian Supreme Leader Ali Khamenei to be ill with prostate cancer. See Pepe Escobar, "An Ill Wind in Iran," *Asia Times* (Hong Kong), March 2, 2007, http://www.atimes.com/atimes/Middle_East/IC02Ak03.html.

26. "Quarterly Iran General Population Poll," Foundation for the Promotion of Democracy, June 13–17, 2008, Excerpts available at http://www.ffpd .org/The_Work_Of_FPD.html.

27. Terror Free Tomorrow, "Polling Iranian Public Opinion: An Unprecedented Nationwide Survey of Iran," October 2007, http://www.terrorfree tomorrow.org/upimagestft/TFT%20Iran%20Survey%20Report.pdf.

28. As cited in Afshin Molavi, "Buying Time in Tehran," *Foreign Affairs* 83, no. 6 (2004): 9.

29. "Inflation Nears 30 Percent in September," Reuters, October 9, 2008, http://www.rferl.org/content/Inflation_In_Iran_Nears_30_Percent_In _September/1328356.html.

30. "Iran's Unemployment Falls To 10.3 Pct–Minister," Reuters, March 31, 2008, http://in.reuters.com/article/asiaCompanyAndMarkets/ idINDAH13987520080331.

31. United Nations Childrens' Fund, "At a Glance: Iran, Islamic Republic Of," n.d., http://www.uniccf.org/infobycountry/iran.html.

32. "Iranian Minister Calls for Temporary Marriages to Fulfill Sexual Desires," Associated Press, June 3, 2007, http://www.foxnews.com/ story/0,2933,277449,00.html.

33. Ibid; Nazila Fathi, "To Regulate Prostitution, Iran Ponders Brothels," *New York Times*, August 28, 2002, http://query.nytimes.com/gst/fullpage .html?res=9404E0DE1F3CF93BA1575BC0A9649C8B63.

34. As cited in Karl Vick, "Opiates of the Iranian People," *Washington Post*, September 23, 2005, A01.

35. Thomas L. Friedman, "An American in Paris," *New York Times*, January 20, 2005, http://www.nytimes.com/2005/01/20/opinion/20friedman.html?hp.

36. "Public Opinion in Iran," worldpublicopinion.org, April 7, 2008, http:// www.worldpublicopinion.org/pipa/pdf/apr08/Iran_Apr08_rpt.pdf.

37. Ibid.

38. "Interview: Sadjadpour: On Iranian Public Support for Tehran's Nuclear Ambitions," March 13, 2006, Council on Foreign Relations, http://www.cfr .org/publication/10100/.

39. See, for example, Azadeh Moaveni, "The Backlash against Iran's Role in Lebanon," *Time*, August 31, 2006, http://www.time.com/time/world/ article/0,8599,1515755,00.html.

40. Eric Hoffer, *The True Believer: Thoughts on the Nature Of Mass Movements* (New York: Harper Perennial Modern Classics, 2002), 17.

41. Ibid., 19.

42. Iranian clerics have proposed officially replacing celebration of the Persian New Year, Norouz, with festivities associated with Ghadir, a Shi'a holiday commemorating the day the Prophet Muhammad named Ali as his successor.

See Omid Memarian, "Ayatollah Khazali Proposed To Ban Nowruz New Year Festivities," *Rooz* (Tehran), July 17, 2007, http://www.roozonline.com/english/archives/2007/07/006125.php. More successful have been their efforts to ban other symbolic Persian holidays, such as Chaharshanbehsouri (the Festival of Fire), which has been officially abolished.

43. Ali Akbar Dareini, "Persian Icons Regain Favor in Modern Iran," *Los Angeles Times*, June 22, 2003, A-5.

44. Ezra HaLevi, "Iran Plans on Destroying Tomb of King Cyrus, Friend of The Jews," Israel National News, January 13, 2008, http://www.israelnational news.com/News/News.aspx/124898.

45. I am grateful to Brian Hosford for calling this story to my attention.

46. Ruhollah Khomeini, *Islamic Government* (Washington, DC: National Strategy Information Center, 1979), 114.

47. Mehdi Khalaji, presentation at the AIPAC National Policy Forum, Chicago, Illinois, October 28, 2008.

48. Vali Nasr, *The Shia Revival: How Conflicts within Islam will Shape the Future* (New York: W.W. Norton, 2007), 71–72.

49. See, for example, Hamza Hedawi, "US–Iraq Pact Poses Test for Iraq's Security Forces," Associated Press, November 17, 2008, http://news.yahoo .com/s/ap/20081117/ap_on_re_mi_ea/ml_iraq.

50. Evgueni K. Novikov, *Central Asian Responses to Radical Islam* (Washington, DC: American Foreign Policy Council, 2006), v–vi.

51. Evgueni K. Novikov, "Counterterrorism, Central Asian Style," *The Journal of International Security Affairs* 9 (2005): 65.

52. Reuven Paz and Moshe Terdman, "Africa: Islam's Inroads," *The Journal of International Security Affairs* 13 (2007): 39.

53. See, for example, Douglas Farah and Richard Schultz, "Al Qaeda's Growing Sanctuary," *Washington Post*, July 14, 2004, A19.

54. "Hassan Al-Turabi: Remaking History," *Al-Ahram Weekly* (Cairo) 794, May 11–17, 2006, http://weekly.ahram.org.eg/2006/794/profile.htm.

55. See Middle East Media Research Institute *Special Dispatch* 1143, April 21, 2006, http://memri.org/bin/articles.cgi?Page=subjects&Area=reform&ID= SP114306.

56. Ibid.

3

MESSAGING TO THE (MUSLIM) MASSES

By now, the idea that the struggle against radical Islam is in large part a battle of ideas has become widely accepted. Our statesmen, diplomats, and political leaders regularly intone that we are engaged in a monumental conflict between freedom and fear, between democratic values and religious totalitarianism, and between individual liberties and religious fiat. But is the United States actively engaging in this struggle? Sadly, all of the available evidence suggests that it is not. Nearly eight years into the fight, America still lacks anything remotely resembling a coherent strategy for competing on the Muslim world's intellectual battlefields. And without one, it has steadily ceded the strategic initiative to its adversaries, who do.

That this state of affairs is counterintuitive is something of an understatement. Even during peacetime, the United States needs the ability to actively communicate its values and policies to the outside world. During a time of conflict, particularly one against intractable ideological adversaries, nothing could be more urgent.

COLD WAR SUCCESS

This lack of communication is all the more surprising because not long ago the United States possessed—and successfully implemented—just such a plan, not once but twice. The first was formulated during the early years of the Cold War, when the United States was struggling for a new and innovative approach to its emerging superpower rivalry with the Soviet Union. As part of this effort, President Harry Truman tasked the policy planning staff of then–Secretary of State Dean Acheson with crafting a new national security paradigm to govern relations with the USSR. Truman approved the resulting document, National Security Council paper 68 (NSC-68), on April 14, 1950, thereby committing the United States to a "worldwide" ideological and political struggle to contain the Soviet Union and Communist ideology. This offensive, NSC-68 made clear, was to include informational measures intended "to reduce the power and influence of the Kremlin inside the Soviet Union and other areas under its control."[1]

Today, NSC-68 is widely recognized as the blueprint for the "containment" strategy that came to dominate U.S. policy toward the Soviet Union during the early decades of the Cold War. Yet its contributions to the field of American strategic influence[2] were no less important. With the implementation of NSC-68, the previously ad hoc covert and overt political warfare initiatives carried out by various U.S. government agencies (not least the CIA and its predecessor, the OSS), were consolidated into a new bureaucracy. The centerpiece of this new structure, established by President Truman in April of 1951 to "develop, coordinate and evaluate the national psychological strategy effort" to influence foreign audiences and opinions, was an interagency working group known as the Psychological Strategy Board (PSB).[3] Subsequent national security directives dramatically expanded the authority of the U.S. military to carry out strategic influence operations—from psychological warfare to propaganda—during peacetime.[4]

Truman's successor, Dwight D. Eisenhower, continued this trend. On Ike's watch, a new entity known as the President's Committee on International Information Activities (PCIIA) was formed. With a broader mandate, the PCIIA set about refining, expanding, and strengthening the initiatives already set into motion by the PSB. From its recommendations, detailed in a comprehensive 1953 report, sprang the organizational structure and authority for national security planning possessed today by the President's National Security Council. Political warfare, in its various permutations, was a central part of that structure.

The second effort was initiated by Ronald Reagan in the early 1980s. In line with his view of U.S.-Soviet relations as an intractable ideological contest, Reagan abandoned the "cold peace" that had set in between the superpowers in favor of a vision for victory against Moscow. In July of 1982, he issued National Security Decision Directive 45 (NSDD 45), setting the stage for a dramatic enhancement of America's international communications presence. "International broadcasting," NSDD 45 declared, "constitutes an important instrument in the national security policy of the United States."[5] This directive dictated that the scope and reach of America's premier instruments of international outreach—the Voice of America (VOA) and Radio Free Europe/Radio Liberty (RFE/RL)—would be expanded and strengthened. (NSDD 45 also spawned a new initiative, known as Radio Marti, aimed at assisting the destabilization and discrediting of Fidel Castro's Cuba.)

Two other edicts followed in close succession. NSDD 77, issued in January of 1983, launched a comprehensive strategic communications campaign against the USSR.[6] This offensive entailed the creation of an elaborate interagency process, overseen by a Special Planning Group at the National Security Council, to "counter totalitarian ideologies and aggressive political action moves undertaken by the Soviet Union or Soviet surrogates." Just over a year later, Reagan bolstered this effort with NSDD 130, which dramatically expanded the range of active U.S. strategic communications activities, reinforcing traditional information instruments such as broadcasting, authorizing new ones (such as the distribution of audio and video cassettes), and reinvigorating the use of psychological operations (PSYOP) by the U.S. military.[7]

The practical effects were far-reaching. With greater funding and technical means, VOA and RFE/RL were able to widen their activities—and their appeal—among the oppressed peoples of the Soviet bloc. Their efforts, in turn, have been credited by experts as playing a key role in successfully winning the Cold War for the West.

LOSING THE PEACE . . .

With the collapse of the Soviet Union, however, American strategic influence became a victim of its own success. The end of the Cold War kindled hopes for a "peace dividend" among many in Washington. Some even spoke of the ultimate victory of liberal capitalism on the world stage.[8] In response, U.S. officials embarked upon a systematic dismantlement of the informational infrastructure that had so successfully communicated American values and ideals to the captive masses behind the Iron Curtain.

Throughout the 1990s, U.S. strategic communications suffered death by a thousand cuts, as important and dynamic programs were progressively eliminated, funding dwindled and the human brain trust that had helped to win the ideological battle against Soviet communism was dispersed. In their place, the United States grew more and more dependent on private media, believing against all available evidence that such outlets could communicate U.S. interests as effectively as could their official counterparts.

The crowning blow came in October 1999, when the United States Information Agency (USIA)—until then the operational nerve center of U.S. public outreach—was formally folded into the State Department as part of new legislation aimed at restructuring and streamlining the nation's public diplomacy effort. That decision, more than any other, can be credited with the current systemic dysfunctions plaguing American public diplomacy.

In place of the USIA, the U.S. government opted to erect a hybrid structure—part bureaucratic and part programmatic—to oversee American outreach. Formally, the U.S. State Department took charge of the country's public affairs, cultural outreach, and international education efforts. Practically, American broadcasting became the bailiwick of the Broadcasting Board of Governors (BBG), a bipartisan oversight panel populated largely by prominent businessmen and media figures.

Two results flowed from this fateful decision. The first is an attrition of strategic vision. During the Cold War, broadcasting was viewed as an integral tool of America's larger public diplomacy effort, and its goal, as then–USIA Director Edward R. Murrow told Congress back in the spring of 1963, was "to further the achievement of U.S. foreign policy objectives."[9] The BBG, however, has taken a rather different view. As one Board member famously put it back in 2002, "We've got to think of ourselves as separate from public diplomacy."[10] Not surprisingly, this perception of the BBG as separate from—and not beholden to—U.S. policy has had a pronounced effect on the way the BBG does business.

The second result is a decline in the reach of America's various instruments of strategic influence. During the Cold War, person-to-person exchanges formed the backbone of U.S. cultural diplomacy, exposing foreign constituencies and emerging activists to American ideas, values, and policies. The result was the cultivation of a generation of political leaders—from Vaclav Havel to Helmut Kohl—who understood, and identified with, the vision underpinning American policies. And yet, in the decade that followed the Soviet collapse, the United States unilaterally stripped itself of the ability to influence post–Cold War political leaders in a similar fashion. When tallied in 2002, the number of academic and cultural exchanges between the United States and foreign nations was found to have been slashed by nearly 40 percent (from 45,000 to 29,000 annually) during the second half of the 1990s alone.[11] Simultaneously, American information centers abroad—once a key resource for foreign publics interested in learning more about the United States—were aggressively scaled down.[12]

If anything, broadcasting initiatives have fared even worse. In their heyday at the height of the Cold War, the combined efforts of the Voice of America and RFE/RL are estimated to have reached as much as 80 percent of the population of Eastern Europe, and half of the citizens of the Soviet Union, every week.[13] In turn, the arguments, ideas, and discussions carried on those outlets empowered an emerging generation of leaders within the Soviet bloc—leaders who, armed with Western values, would emerge to challenge the authority of the Soviet Communist Party. Today, however, America's tools of public outreach have been relegated to the margins of politics in the Muslim and Arab worlds.

Part of this decline undoubtedly has to do with funding. When surveyed close to a year and a half after September 11, the United States was spending, in real terms, about one-third less on public diplomacy than it did during the Cold War.[14] Of that money, only a comparatively small fraction is spent on outreach to the principal area in need of such contact: the Muslim world. (In its 2003 survey, the Advisory Group on Public Diplomacy for the Arab and Muslim World estimated that just one-sixth of the State Department's $600 million public diplomacy budget was spent in majority Muslim countries.[15]) The modest increases to America's public diplomacy and public affairs budgets undertaken by the Bush administration during its term in office have only partially addressed the resulting communications deficit.

But even when America's message manages to penetrate Arab and Muslim society, it often falls on deaf ears. This is largely because, over the past decade, Washington has ceased actively affecting what foreign audiences know or feel about America and its values. Instead, consistent with former BBG Commissioner Norman Pattiz's belief that MTV, rather than American ideals or Soviet corruption, "brought down the Berlin Wall,"[16] American public diplomacy has gravitated to a lighter, music-driven format.

The resulting decline in U.S. strategic influence is hardly surprising. "The more like commercial radio U.S. broadcasting becomes, the less reason it has to exist," former VOA Director Robert Reilly explains. "After all, the image of America created by the popular media is the cliché that often repels much of the world. U.S. broadcasting has the duty to reveal the character of the American people in such a way that the underlying principles of American life are revealed. Music with a sprinkling of news cannot do this."[17]

. . . AND CEDING THE INFORMATIONAL BATTLEGROUND

Little in this sorry picture has changed since September 11. To its credit, the Bush administration grasped early on the importance of political warfare to the new worldwide conflict against the forces of radical Islam. Thus, its formative *National Security Strategy of the United States of America*, released publicly in September 2002, counseled that:

> Just as our diplomatic institutions must adapt so that we can reach out to others, we also need a different and more comprehensive approach to public information efforts that can help people around the world learn about and understand America. The war on terrorism is not a clash of civilizations. It does, however, reveal the clash inside a civilization, a battle for the future of the Muslim world. This is a struggle of ideas and this is an area where America must excel.[18]

As a practical matter, however, the U.S. government did nothing of the sort. To the contrary, even as it professed its commitment to fighting the "war of ideas," the Bush administration voluntarily took itself out of the competition in it.

To be sure, the start of the War on Terror prompted a media reorientation toward the Middle East on the part of the White House. The first step in this process was the establishment in 2002 of Radio Sawa, a flashy radio channel heavily laden with the latest pop music but light on critical analysis and news, to serve as the successor to VOA's lackluster Arabic Service. Two years later, with considerable fanfare, the BBG launched *Alhurra*, a high-profile satellite television station aimed at providing news and analysis for audiences in the Arab and Muslim worlds. The success of these initiatives has been mixed, however. By all accounts, Sawa has a marginal impact on the Middle Eastern political scene, in large part because its format is seen as "fun" but "irrelevant" by locals.[19] *Alhurra*, while more successful, has succumbed in recent times to a corrosive culture of subtle anti-Americanism (manifested through, among other things, ever greater media airtime to terrorists and their sympathizers).[20]

Nor has this reorganization meant more money. Against all logic, funding for U.S. public diplomacy has not risen by any appreciable amount since 2001.[21] And without such additional investments, much of this reorganization has come at the expense of other critical programming. Thus, in early 2007, in an effort to reallocate resources to its Middle Eastern programming, the White House announced a major constriction in the worldwide activities of the Voice of America. These cuts, outlined in the FY2008 foreign operations budget presented by the administration to Congress, included the outright elimination of English-language broadcasts by VOA on every continent except Africa, a cessation of the VOA's Cantonese, Croatian, Greek, Georgian, Thai, and Uzbek services, and a significant reduction in the programming of what was arguably the agency's flagship effort, the VOA Russian service. [22] This evisceration was only delayed by swift action from Congress, which in mid-2007 authorized an emergency support fund to sustain the programming in question, at least temporarily.

The administration's decision left longtime public diplomacy professionals aghast. As eleven former VOA directors pointed in an open letter to the president, such a step—coming at a time when authoritarian regimes such as Russia and Iran were increasing their repression on local media sources, and when unfriendly news outlets such as *al-Jazeera* had ramped up their coverage—was tantamount to strategic surrender. "At this critical moment in the post 9/11 era," they warned, "the United States simply cannot, for its own long term strategic safety and security, unilaterally disarm in the global contest of ideas."[23] Others have been more direct. "The cumulative effect of these cuts alone would be to write-off more than 18 million listeners each week around the world," wrote the Center for Security Policy, a national security think tank. In response, it asked incredulously: "Who could possibly choose voluntarily to eliminate such an audience, much of which is in places critical to the future course of this war?"[24]

Nor has the State Department, now the U.S. government's principal public diplomacy coordinator, fared better. For years, the State Department has floundered without a coherent vision for outreach, under a succession of beleaguered stewards. The first such point-person was Charlotte Beers, a high-powered marketing executive that President Bush appointed to the newly-created post of Under Secretary of State for Public Diplomacy and Public Affairs just one month after the September 11 attacks. Beers entered office with high expectations and an ambitious plan to repackage America in the eyes of foreign audiences. But she would depart just a year-and-a-half later, her marketing scheme for "Brand America" thoroughly discredited by foreign audiences. The reasons were obvious. As one expert put it: "The general approach of advertising is to try to influence an audience with a short attention span by using subliminal messages to affect short-term behavior. It reduces the war of ideas to slogans that are of marginal use in persuading thoughtful people concerning matters of life and death."[25]

Beers's successor, Margaret Tutwiler, lasted even less time and left even less of an impression, fleeing the post in June 2004, just six months after being sworn in. It was not until the installation of Karen Hughes, President Bush's close personal confidante and longtime advisor, that the State Department's sclerotic public diplomacy bureaucracy appeared to be nudged into action. But the resulting strategic plan, the *U.S. National Strategy for Public Diplomacy and Strategic Communication* released by the State Department in December 2006, still left a great deal to be desired. As the U.S. government's internal watchdog, the Government Accountability Office, pointed out in its assessment of the situation in the summer of 2007, the Department of State—whatever its formal strategy—still exhibits serious practical deficiencies in carrying out effective public diplomacy action.[26]

Matters have admittedly improved since. In June 2008, a new under secretary took the helm of the State Department's public outreach efforts. James Glassman, a veteran journalist and author, was selected for the post following a brief but dynamic tenure as chairman of the BBG. Glassman has given hopeful signs of understanding the importance of media to the current struggle, and of the need for a comprehensive coordinated approach to it.[27] Yet, as of this writing, his tenure, and perhaps even his approach, is not expected to long survive the transition to a new government in Washington.

Other corners of the U.S. government have been even harder hit. Pentagon efforts to forge a coherent strategic influence strategy, for example, have been stillborn—a casualty of political pressure and bureaucratic infighting. Such was the case of the Office of Strategic Influence (OSI), established in October 2001 by then–Secretary of Defense Donald Rumsfeld to develop "a full spectrum influence strategy that would result in greater foreign support of U.S. goals and repudiation of terrorists and their methods."[28] But the OSI was plagued with problems from the start; congressional critics lambasted the office, terming it a subversive, unaccountable propaganda unit. Unflattering newspaper accounts did much the same.[29] These attacks took their toll, and in February 2002, just four months after commissioning the OSI, Rumsfeld shuttered the office, declaring it to be "so damaged" as to be unable to "function effectively."[30] In lieu of the OSI, Pentagon planners opted for a lower-profile option, creating the post of Deputy Assistant Secretary of Defense for Public Diplomacy Support. But that position, established on the recommendation of the Defense Science Board, lay vacant for almost a year-and-a-half before accepting its first occupant, former Princeton University associate professor Michael Scott Doran, in 2007.

This rot has been mirrored at the operational level. In the early stages of the War on Terror, United States Central Command (USCENTCOM), the principal combatant command responsible for the greater Middle East, established a Media Engagement Team (MET) to coordinate the informational front of Coalition operations. Launched in August 2005, this small, ad hoc unit, headquartered in Dubai, served as the U.S. military's primary liaison unit with *al-Jazeera*, *al-Arabiya*, and other regional media outlets. But in mid-2007, clashes of personality between some members of the MET and CENTCOM's new commander, Admiral William Fallon, led to its complete dissolution.[31] It was not until General David Petraeus assumed the post of CENTCOM chief in October of 2008, more than a year later, that tentative steps began to be taken to reconstitute this capability. And in its absence, the U.S.-led Coalition compromised its ability to interface with the often-hostile Arab media, a crucial medium in the "battle of ideas" now taking place in the region.

It is only in Iraq that the United States appears to have truly begun to use informational tools as a weapon of war. Building upon the recommendations of the U.S. Army's new *Counterinsurgency Field Manual*, Coalition forces have begun to place greater emphasis on information operations that "exploit inconsistencies in the insurgents' message as well as their excessive use of force or intimidation,"[32] with considerable effect. Yet a survey of political warfare initiatives now underway suggests strongly that this instance of successful strategic influence is still very much the exception rather than the rule.

FROM DEFENSE TO OFFENSE

This disarray has not gone unnoticed. Over the past several years, scores of studies, reports, and assessments have taken stock of America's ability to exert strategic influence abroad.[33] Their conclusions have been practically unanimous. A "process of unilateral disarmament in the weapons of advocacy over the last decade has contributed to widespread hostility toward Americans and left us vulnerable to lethal threats to our interests and our safety," the Advisory Group on Public Diplomacy for the Arab and Muslim World chaired by former U.S. ambassador to Syria Edward Djerejian declared in its October 2003 report.[34] Others have been even more blunt. America's strategic communications are "in crisis," the Pentagon's elite Defense Science Board warned in 2004, and "must be transformed with a strength of purpose that matches our commitment to diplomacy, defense, intelligence, law enforcement, and homeland security."[35]

How can the United States do so? By now, many policymakers have spoken about the "battle of ideas" that must be waged against our adversaries, and intoned the importance of winning "hearts and minds" in the Arab and Muslim worlds. But few actually know what this means. Fewer still understand how such a goal can be achieved in the new strategic environment now confronting the United States. As one astute observer put it, "The U.S. has a 'secret weapon' of sorts that is so secret that policymakers don't seem to appreciate the sum of its parts."[36] That secret weapon is a spectrum of informational disciplines which, if properly harnessed, hold the power to shape foreign perceptions and help the United States dominate the intellectual battlefield of our struggle against radical Islam. What has been missing so far is a coordinated plan for doing so.

Such a plan must start with a recalibrated American message. During the Cold War, the "battle of ideas" waged by Washington was largely an external one—a struggle between Western values and Communist ideology. The United States and its allies emerged victorious, in large part because they succeeded in convincing the captive nations of the Soviet bloc of the moral and practical bankruptcy of the Soviet system.

Today, the nature of the challenge is very different. The United States is indeed attempting to wage an external campaign to counter the propaganda and political rhetoric of al-Qaeda and other radicals—albeit not very well, by all accounts. Simultaneously, however, it also needs to work *within* the world of Islam, diluting the appeal of extremist ideology to "undecided voters," diminishing the regional stature and legitimacy of religious radicals, and exacerbating the fissures between these forces and the societies in which they operate.

So far, the United States has done nothing of the sort. For the past several years, American strategic communications have focused predominantly on the external informational struggle against the terrorists, rather than the internal one. In doing so, the U.S. government has unconsciously reverted to Cold War thinking about the need to demonstrate the superiority of American values. And that, as has become exceedingly clear, constitutes a major strategic blunder. "Today we reflexively compare Muslim 'masses' to those oppressed under Soviet rule," the Defense Science Board pointed out in its 2004 report on the subject. But "[t]here is no yearning-to-be-liberated-by-the-U.S. groundswell among Muslim societies—*except to be liberated perhaps from what they see as apostate tyrannies that the U.S. so determinedly promotes and defends.* [emphasis added]."[37] In other words, American values, though intrinsic to U.S. public diplomacy, have far less operational value in today's strategic environment than they did some three decades ago. The Muslim world is not the Soviet Union, and the constituencies there have very different perceptions of the United States, its goals, and its interests.

Clarifying the resulting misconceptions can and should be a key part of America's message. Equally important, however, is recalibrating the thrust of U.S strategic communications. Rather than attempt to convince skeptical Muslim audiences of our good intentions, Washington's goal should be "to win anti-democratic and very hostile elements away from the hard core," explains J. Michael Waller of the Institute of World Politics. After all, "[w]e are not trying to persuade them of the virtues of democracy, the liberation of women, or alternate lifestyles. We are not necessarily trying to make them our friends. We don't expect expressions of gratitude. We are simply appealing to their own interests as the enemy of their enemy."[38]

Other experts concur. "While some proportion of our terrorist opponents may indeed be undeterrable, there is also likely to be significant variation in their susceptibility to external messages," according to the Naval War College's Carnes Lord. "One such message, delivered by some combination of force and persuasive speech, might be a simple one: 'your cause is futile.'"[39]

ADOPTING A CAMPAIGN FOOTING

In the early 1960s, while he languished in prison in Gamal Abdel Nasser's Egypt, Sayyid Qutb, the intellectual father of modern militant Islam, released his manifesto, entitled *Ma'alim fi al-Tariq* (Milestones). Qutb, an Egyptian intellectual and sometime academic, had become radicalized during his formal education in the 1930s and 1940s, when he spent several years studying in the United States and saw firsthand what he deemed the "corruption" of the West. Upon his return to Egypt, Qutb drifted more and more deeply into radical Islam, becoming a power broker in the country's most influential Islamist movement, the Muslim Brotherhood.[40] By the time *Milestones* was published, Qutb had formulated his views about the ungodliness of the West, the supremacy of *sharia* law, and the need for armed struggle to root out *jahiliyya* (disbelief).

For years, these views would go unchallenged. The first popular English-language translation of *Milestones* did not enter circulation until the early 1980s.[41] And, as a result, for over a decade-and-a-half, Qutb's ideas about the irreconcilability of Western values and Islamic ideals circulated unchallenged throughout the Middle East. The damage done was incalculable; without a countervailing Western message, many in the Muslim and Arab worlds grew to believe Qutb's depiction of the United States and Europe, and embrace his call for their overthrow.

During the decades when America was preoccupied with the struggle against Soviet communism, this kind of failure could perhaps have been forgiven. Today, however, it cannot be. The proliferation of continuous, instantaneous media and the Internet has given radical Islam's ideologues far greater ability to disseminate their message to followers and potential adherents alike. And they are actively exploiting this new medium. Through a steady diet of public broadcasts, Internet messaging, and multimedia outreach, al-Qaeda has continued to shape global events despite its dislocation from its traditional safe haven of Afghanistan.

If the bin Laden network is taking seriously the battle for "hearts and minds," the United States so far is not. U.S. policy experts and government officials studiously translate and dissect the public messages of Osama bin Laden and his lieutenants. Rarely if ever, though, has the United States opted to discredit either the message or the messenger—let alone done so in a timely manner.

This is a critical mistake. "In an asymmetric conflict," writes one specialist, "we simply cannot allow an information vacuum to develop because it will be filled with the gossip and lies of the insurgents and extremists."[42] Instead, the United States needs to seize the initiative, helping to shape the terms of the ideological landscape in the current conflict through a constant informational offensive calibrated to key target audiences.

On this score, U.S. officials could learn much from the methodology and pace of U.S. political campaigns, where image warfare is an art form, and where every claim, assertion, and barb made by a political opponent—no matter how petty—is answered quickly and resolutely. In the past, a number of studies have recommended the United States government adopt such a "campaign-style" approach,[43] with little apparent impact. And because it has not adopted such a footing, Washington has progressively ceded the informational initiative in an increasingly fast-moving communications battlespace.

Tilting the balance in its favor requires the United States to assume a proactive approach to countering enemy disinformation, and in providing the proper prism for combatants and civilians alike to view the current conflict. This necessitates building the institutional mechanisms—interagency groups, counterpropaganda units, and political crisis teams—to operationalize such a rapid response effort. And in Washington's corridors of power, it requires senior management that views such strategic communication as intrinsic to the war effort, rather than incidental to it.

ORGANIZING FOR SUCCESS

None of this will be possible without a structural reorganization of the way the United States carries out strategic influence. As experts have pointed out, much of the incoherence plaguing American public outreach today stems from a failure of organization.[44] During the decades of the Cold War, the United States Information Agency (USIA) served as the front line of U.S. strategic communications, implementing and then overseeing American soft power strategy against the USSR. Not so now. The abolition of the USIA in 1999 left American public outreach without a coherent organizing body. And without one, the various strains of American strategic influence have evolved in different directions.

The sole bright spot in this otherwise gloomy picture is information operations (IO). The military application of public diplomacy has experienced a renaissance, driven in large part by the Pentagon's new focus on unconventional warfare (UW). But even here, IO is not pursued in its own right, as a nonkinetic adjunct to "direct action," but is slaved to the counterinsurgency strategy now being implemented in Iraq.

Needless to say, such a state of affairs is unacceptable. The White House needs to do a far better job of ensuring that its message is communicated to the outside world. And that requires reuniting these various elements into a new informational architecture capable of harnessing the tools of American strategic influence in the "war of ideas" now taking place in the Muslim and Arab worlds.

In its 2004 study, the Defense Science Board made the case for a "permanent strategic communication structure" within the U.S. National Security Council, complete with the creation of the post of "Deputy National Security Advisor for Strategic Communication" and the establishment of an interagency Strategic Communication Committee with "authority to assign responsibilities and plan the work of departments and agencies . . . [and] shape strategic communication budget priorities."[45] Others have taken an even more radical approach; the "Strategic Communications Act of 2008," introduced in September 2008 by Sen. Sam Brownback (R-KS), recommends the creation of a completely new federal agency, the National Center for Strategic Communications, with similar functions and powers to the now-defunct USIA.[46]

These proposals each have much to commend them. Ultimately, however, the future shape of the U.S. strategic communications effort will be decided by the White House itself. But whatever form it chooses, serious investments in two concrete areas will be required.

The first is leadership. As one veteran government official has succinctly summarized, "the most fundamental problem" with U.S. public diplomacy "is that no one in the U.S. is in charge. Each U.S. government agency currently has their own informational program, but the bureaucracy as a whole lacks a senior official with the authority to integrate these efforts."[47] Without it, the various agencies responsible for communicating America's message to the world have succumbed to bureaucratic infighting, funding battles, and conflicting mandates.

The closest thing the White House currently has to such a function is the post of Under Secretary of State for Public Diplomacy and Public

Affairs. But while some have heaped praise upon the position—Senator Joseph Lieberman famously identified it as the "the closest thing to a supreme allied commander in the war of ideas" that currently exists in Washington[48]—the reality is that the position is limited in scope and authority in several key respects. What is needed, therefore, is a real strategic communications "czar," a single individual with primary responsibility for truly harnessing the tools of American strategic influence over the length and breadth of the governmental bureaucracy.

The second is resources. "You get what you pay for," the old saying goes, and the arena of strategic influence is no different. By any yardstick, America's current investment in communicating its ideas and policies to the outside world remains minimal. For the 2008 fiscal year, America's total combined public diplomacy spending stood at some $1.15 billion—or roughly a tenth of the State Department's total budget.[49] Of that sum, just 7.5 percent, $154 million, was allocated for public outreach toward the Middle East, the principal theater of operations in the struggle against radical Islam.[50]

Not surprisingly, given this shortfall, the United States has been forced to progressively cede the communications battlespace to its more agile, more innovative, and more resourceful adversaries. "The coalition has failed to counter enemy propaganda either by responding rapidly with effective counter messages or by proactively challenging the messages, methods, and ideology that the insurgents and extremists promote and exploit," one political warfare practitioner has lamented.[51] If it hopes to be able to defeat the ideology of its adversaries, the United States must first be able to match—or, better yet, to exceed—the volume of their message. And that necessarily means committing far greater resources than currently allocated to public diplomacy and strategic communications.

PUSHING BACK

The stakes could not be any higher. By any yardstick, the number of extremists now actively engaged in warfare against the United States and its allies is minuscule. The State Department's 2007 *Country Reports on Terrorism* identifies some twenty-three Islamist terrorist groups, with a combined strength of fewer than one hundred thousand active operatives.[52] But, with the Muslim world now estimated at close to a fifth of humanity, and with no shortage of privation and discontent among Muslim communities in the Middle East and Africa, the pool of potential recruits to the cause of radical Islam, in either its Shi'a or Sunni variants, is virtually limitless.

America's ideological adversaries understand this very well, and have made strategic outreach a key priority. Experts estimate that the Kingdom of Saudi Arabia alone has spent as much as $4 billion annually for the past two decades to spread its official state ideology, Wahhabi Islam.[53] Other countries, such as Iran, are likewise investing heavily in shaping the political environments in places such as Afghanistan and Iraq through communications mediums.[54] Non-state actors—from al-Qaeda to Hezbollah to insurgents in Iraq—are also getting into the "hearts and minds" game, much to the detriment of America's message abroad.

So far, Washington has not fielded a robust response to this informational offensive. Rather, it has contented itself with advocating the "lasting diversion" of foreign audiences away from radical Islamist ideology toward "entertainment, culture, literature, music technology, sports, education, business and culture, in addition to politics and religion."[55] As a tactic, such an approach has much to commend it. As a long-term strategy, however, the United States will need to go much further. If it hopes to achieve what military planners term "battlefield dominance" in the war of ideas, the United States will need to harness its tools of strategic influence into a coordinated strategy that engages the Muslim world while simultaneously discrediting and marginalizing the message of the extremists attempting to hijack it.

NOTES

1. White House, National Security Council, *NSC 68: United States Objectives and Programs for National Security*, April 14, 1950, http://www.fas.org/irp/offdocs/nsc-hst/nsc-68.htm.

2. Strategic influence (used here interchangeably with political warfare) has been broadly defined by scholars and practitioners as government informational activities designed to influence opinions, attitudes, and behavior of foreign groups in ways that will promote U.S. interests. It encompasses the disciplines of public affairs, public diplomacy, and strategic communications, as well as its military applications: information operations and psychological operations (PSYOP). See, for example, Carnes Lord, *Losing Hearts and Minds?*

Public Diplomacy and Strategic Influence in the Age of Terror (Westport, CT: Praeger, 2006), 8.

3. Susan L. Gough, "The Evolution of Strategic Influence," United States Army War College Strategy Research Project, April 7, 2003, 10.

4. Ibid.

5. White House, National Security Decision Directive 45, "United States International Broadcasting," July 15, 1982, http://www.fas.org/irp/offdocs/nsdd/nsdd-045.htm.

6. White House, National Security Decision Directive 77, "Management of Public Diplomacy Relative to National Security," January 14, 1983. (author's collection)

7. White House, National Security Decision Directive 130, "U.S. International Information Policy," March 6, 1984, as reprinted in J. Michael Waller, ed. *The Public Diplomacy Reader* (Washington, DC: Institute of World Politics Press, 2007), 299–303.

8. See, for example, Francis Fukuyama, *The End of History and the Last Man* (New York: Harper Perennial, 1993).

9. The Honorable Edward R. Murrow, Statement before the U.S. House of Representatives Subcommittee on International Organizations and Movements, March 28, 1963, as cited in Waller, *The Public Diplomacy Reader*, 25.

10. Edward Kaufman, as cited in Glenn Hauser, ed., *DX Listening Digest* 2-142, September 11, 2002, http://www.worldofradio.com/dxld2142.txt.

11. U.S. Advisory Commission on Public Diplomacy, *Building America's Public Diplomacy through a Reformed Structure and Additional Resources* (Washington, DC: U.S. Department of State, 2002), 10.

12. Stephen Johnson and Helle Dale, "How to Reinvigorate U.S. Public Diplomacy," Heritage Foundation *Backgrounder* 1645(April 2003): 4

13. Anthony J. Blinken, "Winning the War of Ideas," *The Washington Quarterly* 25, no. 2 (2002): 105.

14. Advisory Commission for Public Diplomacy Chairman Harold Pachios, remarks at the Newhouse School of Communication at Syracuse University, Syracuse, New York, January 28, 2003, http://www.state.gov/r/adcompd/rls/19104.htm.

15. *Changing Minds, Winning Peace: A New Strategic Direction for U.S. Public Diplomacy in the Arab & Muslim World*, Advisory Group on Public Diplomacy for the Arab and Muslim World, October 1, 2003, 26.

16. As cited in "The Sound of America," *New Yorker*, February 18 and 25, 2002, http://www.newyorker.com/talk/content/articles/020218ta_talk_mayer.

17. Robert Reilly, "Winning the War of Ideas," *Claremont Review of Books* 7, no. 3 (2007): 35–37.

18. White House, *National Security Strategy of the United States of America*, September 2002, 31.

19. See, for example, Robert R. Reilly, "Britney vs. the Terrorists," *Washington Post*, February 9, 2007, A19.

20. See, for example, Joel Mowbray, "Television Takeover," *Wall Street Journal*, March 18, 2007, http://www.opinionjournal.com/editorial/feature .html?id=110009801.

21. The Bush administration's 2003 budget allocated $1.15 billion for public diplomacy activities, divided more or less evenly between the Broadcasting Board of Governors ($557 million) and State Department educational and cultural initiatives ($593 million). Five years later, the Administration's 2008 budget contained a greater share ($668 million) for the BBG, and a smaller one ($486 million) for State Department efforts, but the total was the same: $1.15 billion. Jess T. Ford, Testimony Before the U.S. House of Representatives Committee on Government Reform Subcommittee on National Security, Emerging Threats, and International Relations, February 10, 2004, http://ics.leeds.ac.uk/ papers/pmt/exhibits/1422/Ford.pdf; White House, "Fact Sheet: FY2008 Budget for State and International Programs," February 5, 2007, http://www.america .gov/st/texttrans-english/2007/February/20070205143128eaifas0.1317102.html.

22. Press release, "Former VOA Directors Appeal for Reversal of Plan to Reduce Network's Presence on the World's Radio Airwaves," March 5, 2007, http://www.publicdiplomacy.org/78.htm.

23. Ibid.

24. "Soft Power Unplugged," Center for Security Policy *Decision Brief*, June 5, 2007, http://www.centerforsecuritypolicy.org/Modules/NewsManager/ ShowSectionNews.aspx?CategoryID=56&SubCategoryID=71&NewsID=14104.

25. Reilly, "Winning the War of Ideas."

26. United States Government Accountability Office, "U.S. Public Diplomacy: Actions Needed to Improve Strategic Use and Coordination of Research," Report to the Ranking Member, Committee on Foreign Relations, U.S. Senate, GAO-07-904, July 2007, http://www.gao.gov/new.items/d07904.pdf.

27. See James K. Glassman, "Media Is Half The Battle," *Wall Street Journal*, September 17, 2007, http://www.aei.org/publications/filter.all,pubID.26809/ pub_detail.asp.

28. *Department of Defense Responses to Senator Carl Levin*, cited in Office of the Under Secretary of Defense for Acquisition, Technology, and Logistics, *Report of the Defense Science Board on Strategic Communications*, September 2004, 24.

29. See, for example, James Dao and Eric Schmitt, "Pentagon Readies Efforts to Sway Sentiment Abroad," *New York Times*, February 19, 2002, http://query.nytimes .com/gst/fullpage.html?res=9C06EFD71F3FF93AA25751C0A9649C8B63.

30. Eric Schmitt and James Dao, "A 'Damaged' Information Office is Declared Closed by Rumsfeld," *New York Times*, February 27, 2002, http://query.nytimes .com/gst/fullpage.html?res=9906E6DB1431F934A15751C0A9649C8B63.

31. Author's interviews with CENTCOM officials, Washington, DC, and Tampa, Florida, November–December 2007 and February 2008.

32. United States Department of the Army, "Counterinsurgency," *Field Manual* No. 3-24, December 2006, 1–18, http://www.fas.org/irp/doddir/army/fm3-24.pdf.

33. See, for example, *Finding America's Voice: A Strategy for Reinvigorating U.S. Public Diplomacy,* (New York: Council on Foreign Relations, 2003); Stephen Johnson and Helle Dale, "How to Reinvigorate U.S. Public Diplomacy," Heritage Foundation *Backgrounder* no. 1645, April 2003; and, most recently, U.S. Department of Defense, Office of the Under Secretary of Defense for Acquisition, Technology and Logistics, *Report of the Defense Science Board Task Force on Strategic Communication,* September 2004.

34. *Changing Minds, Winning Peace: A New Strategic Direction for U.S. Public Diplomacy in the Arab & Muslim World,* 13.

35. *Report of the Defense Science Board on Strategic Communications,* 2.

36. J. Michael Waller, *Fighting the War of Ideas Like a Real War* (Washington, DC: Institute of World Politics Press, 2007), 14.

37. *Report of the Defense Science Board on Strategic Communications,* 37. Emphasis in original.

38. Waller, *Fighting the War of Ideas Like a Real War,* 35.

39. Lord, *Losing Hearts and Minds?,* 38.

40. Paul Berman, "The Philosopher of Islamic Terror," *New York Times Magazine,* March 23, 2003, http://www.nytimes.com/2003/03/23/magazine/23GURU.html.

41. The first popularly available English language translation of *Milestones* is believed to be the one published by the Cedar Rapids-based Mother Mosque Foundation in 1981.

42. Andrew Garfield, "Recovering the Lost Art of Counterpropaganda: An Assessment of the War in Iraq," as reprinted in Waller, *The Public Diplomacy Reader,* 336.

43. See, for example, United States Government Accountability Office, *U.S. Public Diplomacy: Strategic Planning Efforts Have Improved, but Agencies Face Significant Implementation Challenges,* GAO 07-795-T, April 26, 2007, http://www.gao.gov/new.items/d07795t.pdf. See also Blinken, "Winning the War of Ideas," 109.

44. See, for example, Lord, *Losing Hearts and Minds?* 65–72.

45. *Report of the Defense Science Board on Strategic Communications,* 65.

46. "Strategic Communications Act of 2008," S. 3546, 109th Congress, introduced September 23, 2008.

47. William Boykin, "Al-Qaeda: Enduring Appeal," *The Journal of International Security Affairs* 15 (2008): 76.

48. As cited in "Official: U.S. Enemies 'Eating Our Lunch' Online," CNN, January 30, 2008, http://www.cnn.com/2008/POLITICS/01/30/internet.pr.failure/.

49. White House Fact Sheet, "Bush's FY2008 Budget for State and International Program," February 5, 2007, http://usinfo.state.gov/xarchives/display.html?p=texttrans-english&y=2007&m=February&x=20070205143128eaifas0.1317102.

50. Correspondence from the Office of the Deputy Assistant Secretary for Budget and Planning, U.S. Department of State, May 19, 2008 (author's collection). Correspondence from the White House Office of Management and Budget, December 1, 2008 (author's collection).

51. Andrew Garfield, "The U.S. Counter-Propaganda Failure in Iraq," *Middle East Quarterly* 14, no. 4 (2007), http://www.meforum.org/article/1753.

52. Extrapolated from "Chapter 6—Terrorist Organizations," in U.S. Department of State, Office of the Coordinator of Counterterrorism, *Country Reports on Terrorism 2007* (Washington, DC: U.S. Department of State, April 2008), http://www.state.gov/s/ct/rls/crt/2007/103714.htm.

53. See, for example, Alex Alexiev, "The End of an Alliance," *National Review* 54, no. 20, (2002): 38–42.

54. See, for example, Garfield, "The U.S. Counter-Propaganda Failure in Iraq."

55. James Glassman, address before the Washington Institute for Near East Policy, July 8, 2008, http://www.washingtoninstitute.org/templateC07.php?CID=408.

ECONOMIC
AREA DENIAL

In the early morning hours of November 7, 2001, federal agents with the U.S. Customs Service, the Internal Revenue Service, the Treasury Department's Office of Foreign Assets Control, and the Federal Bureau of Investigation descended upon a series of businesses in Boston; Seattle; Minneapolis; Columbus, Ohio; and Alexandria and Falls Church, Virginia. Their targets were firms suspected of involvement in an informal global financial transfer system known as "Al Barakat," believed to be a key financial conduit to al-Qaeda.

The "Al Barakat" raid was the opening salvo in the U.S. government's post–September 11 effort to target the economic lifeblood of al-Qaeda and other terrorist organizations. In the years since, aided by the creation of a massive interagency task force known as Operation Green Quest and new presidential authorities dramatically expanding the power of U.S. government agencies to seek out and target terrorist funds, that offensive has made major progress. When tallied in 2007, the U.S. government was estimated to have seized some $265 million in al-Qaeda assets, roughly equivalent to nine years of operating expenses for the terror group. It has also managed to freeze millions in funds from other terrorist groups to date.[1] This coordinated, multifaceted strategy, according to experts, has made the effort to combat terrorism financing "one of the few areas of government success" in our overall war effort.[2]

The financial front in our current struggle has not been without its challenges, however. America's efforts have been constrained by the comparatively low cost of financing and carrying out terror attacks (according to the 9/11 Commission, the cost of the September 11 attacks was just $400,000 to $500,000[3]) as well as by the bewildering array of mechanisms used by contemporary terrorist groups, many of which are difficult to trace and even harder to halt. Perhaps most significant, however, has been our failure thus far make the international economy as a whole inhospitable to exploitation by terrorist groups and radical regimes. In military terms, this sort of strategy is called "area denial," and it is essential if the West hopes to take the offensive on the financial battlefield of the current war.

BUYING IN

Such an approach must start with greater investment from the American people. In the days after September 11, as the U.S. government mobilized its response to al-Qaeda, the American public looked to Washington for guidance. Millions had witnessed the horrific attacks on New York and Washington. They felt the same sense of deep shock and lingering outrage at the atrocities that had been perpetrated against ordinary civilians by remorseless religious radicals. And, in response, they wanted to know what they could do to help.

But the answer never came. From the outset, the Bush administration showed little interest in engaging—or harnessing—the American public as part of its war effort. Quite the contrary; far from mobilizing Americans to sacrifice, the White House wanted little more than for the public to continue carrying on business as usual.

That decision has been a fateful one. Practically every international conflict in which the United States has become involved over the past century has been accompanied by a social and economic investment of some sort on the part of the American public. In those conflicts where it has managed to properly harness this popular support, the United States has persevered. This was true in 1917, when America's entry into World War I generated a surge in industrial production and a major economic plan on the part of the Wilson administration,[4] and again during World War II, which saw an even more extraordinary economic, political, and social mobilization among ordinary Americans, who assumed the role of "citizen soldiers" to help the fight against the Axis powers through their purchases, investments, and volunteerism.

It is decidedly not the case today, however. Nearly eight years into our current struggle, few Americans feel directly involved in the conflict—or invested in it. Moreover, this disconnect has only deepened as the events of September 11 recede further into memory. And as a result, a dangerous cleavage has emerged in American society, a rift between those now on the front lines of the fight against radical Islam and ordinary Americans, who are hard pressed to remember that there is, in fact, a conflict underway. As one retired general observed to the *Christian Science Monitor* not long ago: "Marines are at war, America is at the mall."[5]

If it aspires to victory in the current conflict, the United States will need to reverse this perception. In order to do so, it will have to better understand—and then more effectively exploit—the ability of American citizens, businesses, and corporations to play a positive role in denying terrorists the economic quarter they require in order to remain in business.

INTERNATIONALIZING GLOBAL SECURITY RISK

There's a great deal of truth to the saying that "if the U.S. economy sneezes, the rest of the world catches a cold." With roughly half of all global capital flowing through U.S. markets on any given day, America has a quasi-monopoly on global commerce—and significant influence over companies and banks from around the world that rely on U.S. financial channels. The question is how the U.S. can leverage this comparative advantage to make big business an ally in the fight against terrorism.

Some of the seeds for doing so were sown even before September 11. In May of 2001, the Securities and Exchange Commission took a giant leap in this direction when it confirmed to Congress that, in its opinion, "[t]he fact that a foreign company is doing material business with a country, government, or entity on [the U.S. Treasury Department's] sanctions list" should significantly impact "a reasonable investor's decision about whether to invest in that company."[6] Although the determination was made initially from a strictly financial perspective, the subsequent attacks on New York and Washington helped underscore how international business, finance, and national security could intersect and provide new points of leverage.

Lawmakers took notice. Three years later, Congress passed the Fiscal Year 2004 Consolidated Appropriations Act, which included a mandate for the SEC to establish a dedicated Office of Global Security Risk. The goal of the new initiative was seemingly modest: to ensure proper disclosure from companies regarding their ties to sanctioned states, including those that sponsored terrorism. Over time, however, the strategic value of the first regulation to combine geopolitics and corporate governance became clear.[7]

Among the general public, the development barely registered. But in the financial world, its impact was nothing short of earth-shattering. For decades, the economic and political worlds had operated by and large separately and independently. Corporations did not expect to be held accountable for the conduct of the countries with which they did business, especially when that business was technically legal. To these elites, the SEC's new focus on global security "risk"—and the implicit threat of adverse consequences from investors should a company be found to be engaged in commerce with terror-sponsoring or supporting states—was a clear signal that they could no longer expect to go about their business as usual.

Their worries were well founded, for the risk to the corporate reputation and share value of companies if they are disclosed to be associating with sanctioned countries is a real one. Between 1998 and 2004, for example, Canada's Talisman Energy came under tremendous criticism for its investments in the Sudan, which fostered popular perceptions that the company was complicit in genocide there. The bad publicity had a significant impact; in 2004, Talisman caved to public and shareholder pressure and sold off all of its business interests in Sudan.[8] Increasingly, a range of companies are starting to take notice as well. In October 2007, no less than Russia's second-largest oil company, Lukoil, preemptively suspended its development work in Iran's massive Anaran oil field on fears that its activities could make it a financial target in the unfolding international confrontation with the Islamic Republic over its nuclear program.[9] These examples, and others, highlight the power of market forces to change corporate behavior.

In the years since the idea of "global security risk" became more mainstream, its particular melding of business and international security has spawned the emergence of a new financial trend—terror-free investing. It is predicated upon the understanding that, as a result of existing U.S. government regulations, few U.S. firms today do business directly with state sponsors of terrorism such as Iran, Sudan, Syria, and North Korea. But the American public continues to heavily subsidize these regimes indirectly, via investments in foreign corporations and conglomerates that do. Terror-free investing seeks to raise awareness of these corrosive business connections, and to prompt mutual funds, personal investors, and public pension funds, among others, to scale back their involvement with such companies. To this end, terror-free investment practitioners have developed sophisticated tools to screen companies for their "exposure" on this front, and modeled alternative, terror-free investment portfolios that promise competitive rates of return.[10]

The stakes involved in this enterprise are enormous. Experts estimate that there are currently over six hundred publicly traded companies with such business ties, and that the total net value of this terror-linked business runs into the hundreds of billions of dollars.[11] All of which goes a long way toward explaining why many think that terror-free investing, if harnessed properly, can serve as a "formidable force-multiplier" in the fight against terrorism.[12] It highlights the risks companies take by doing business in these countries, and seeks to leverage the resulting reputational risk and decline in share value into coercing companies to exit.

And yet, terror-free investing and its adjunct, divestment, are gathering steam today not because of government endorsement, but in spite of it. So far, the U.S. government has made only nominal steps to institutionalize global security risk as a commercial and trade standard. And it has proven itself to be downright ambivalent about the idea of divestment against countries such as Iran, despite the clear economic benefits the approach can have on the economic dimension of our war effort.[13]

To its credit, the new administration appears more predisposed to implementing such economic warfare tools. During the 2008 presidential election, Senator Barack Obama unequivocally emphasized the need to harness divestment as an economic tool against the regime in Tehran.[14] If it hopes to send a clear signal to multinational companies that they can no longer carry out business as usual with terror-sponsoring regimes, however, his administration now needs to translate these words into real action that strengthens and widens the global security risk standard as it applies to corporate behavior, and expands the use of divestment to ensure that willing risk takers face the consequences.

MAKING MARKET COMPETITION WORK FOR AMERICA

Another area where the United States has fallen short is in its failure to mount a serious economic challenge to terrorist groups on a grassroots level.

Take Lebanon. Today Hezbollah, the Shi'ite militia established by Iran's Revolutionary Guard in the early 1980s, operates as a full-fledged party, with direct control or influence over more than a fifth of the seats in the country's 128-member parliament and major leverage over its political direction.[15] In the country's south, it is also much more. In the wake of Israel's withdrawal from southern Lebanon in May 2000, the group managed to leverage the Lebanese government's weakness to create a virtual state-within-a-state in the territory once occupied by Israeli forces. Now, in that 350-square-mile swath of land, the Islamist movement—and not the authorities in Beirut—operates as the unquestioned law of the land, responsible for everything from social services to sanitation to medicine.[16]

This model can be seen in the Sunni world as well. To be sure, groups such as al-Qaeda have tended to reject the idea of representative governance completely. Thus, the unexpected victory of the Hamas movement in the January 2006 Palestinian elections famously garnered a warning from al-Qaeda's chief ideologue, Ayman al-Zawahiri, that "power is not an end in itself, but simply a stage on the path of implementing *sharia* law."[17] But, in places where governmental authority has faltered, these groups have been quick to exploit the political vacuum that has resulted. This was the case in Afghanistan prior to September 11, where the ideological synergy between the bin Laden network and its Taliban hosts—and the relative political weakness of the latter—allowed al-Qaeda to establish a safe haven from where it could plan and execute attacks against the West.[18] It is much the same today across the border in Pakistan's unruly northwest, where the Federally Administered Tribal Areas remain outside of Islamabad's reach and where, aided by this lack of central control, Sunni Islamic radicals—including, potentially, Osama bin Laden himself—have put down significant roots.

They have done so virtually unchallenged, either politically or ideologically. Intimidated and politically weak, the governments in Beirut, Islamabad, and beyond have allowed such radicals to seize and retain local control without serious opposition. And without real "market competition," the ideology of these groups has proliferated, reinforced by their ubiquitous social welfare, educational, and charitable activities.

The United States has the ability to significantly alter this equation. With roughly $26 billion in foreign aid provided annually to more than 150 nations, America is among the planet's most generous philanthropists.[19] Since September 11, the State Department, for instance, has expended over $5 billion in economic, humanitarian, and security assistance to Pakistan alone.[20] So far, however, these funds have not been used to seriously foster competition with Hezbollah, al-Qaeda, and other radicals in the places where they operate and with the people that look to them for support and sustenance. Rather, since at least the 1970s, America has followed an even-handed approach in its foreign economic assistance, seeing itself as an "honest broker" for, and simultaneously aloof from, the political turf wars taking place throughout the Middle East and beyond.[21] And today, despite the gravity of the current conflict, the U.S. still tends to treat the aid that it disburses to the international community as the foreign policy equivalent of a free lunch.

It was not always this way. In the aftermath of World War II, with the political fate of Europe at stake, the United States launched the European Recovery Program, better known as the Marshall Plan. Between 1948 and 1952, that initiative distributed some $13 billion in direct aid, loan guarantees, and grants for the postwar reconstruction of the Old Continent. In the process, it laid the economic foundation for liberal democratic values, individual freedoms, and political liberty in much of what is now the European Union.

The success of the Marshall Plan begat other economic aid ventures, and the next decade saw the United States expand its geopolitical influence throughout Asia via investments in places like Taiwan, South Korea, and Vietnam.[22] So successful were these early initiatives that Congress in 1961 passed the Foreign Assistance Act, creating the U.S. Agency for International Development (USAID) and entrenching foreign aid as a key element of U.S. foreign policy. The goal, as president John F. Kennedy outlined in 1963, was an early Cold War version of economic area denial, with foreign aid serving as a "vital tool" in America's efforts "to hold back communism in Europe and now also in Asia and elsewhere."[23]

Today, the U.S. government desperately needs to return to just such an approach, one that selects clear winners and losers—and which aids the former while disadvantaging the latter. Through steps such as the establishment of parallel educational institutions, hospitals, and social service organs, the United States can force terrorist groups to do something they currently do not have to: compete in the social "marketplace," and pit their ideas and dollars against those of the United States.

To be sure, many initiatives of this sort are today being implemented throughout the world by a range of U.S. government agencies. But, hampered by America's hesitance to be seen as a meddler in internal affairs, they do so without sufficiently exploiting opportunities to leverage them as part of the ideological struggle in what former CIA director R. James Woolsey has termed the "long war of the 21st century."[24] Indeed, to the extent that proposals have been put forward to do so in places like Iraq, they have been explicitly vetoed by those at home who prefer a status quo approach to both foreign aid and counterterrorism.[25]

This constitutes a fatal error. The United States clearly has a stake in the various political and ideological battles taking place from the greater Middle East to the Horn of Africa. To a large degree, the outcome of those struggles will determine whether those countries emerge as America's allies in the struggle against radical Islam, or as its mortal enemies. As such, Washington has every reason to put its money where its mouth is, and leverage its economic investment into a tool of real ideological competition and change.

TARGET: SHARIA FINANCE

At the same time, the United States will need greater awareness and understanding of the emerging economic trends that could give sustenance to its adversaries in this long war.

Of these, far and away the most potentially significant is *sharia*-compliant finance. Over the past two years, this concept has been actively promoted by Middle Eastern officials and Muslim advocates, who have urged the creation of "more Islamic investment opportunities" in the West.[26] And U.S. financial institutions, driven by the lure of Gulf oil wealth, have responded. When surveyed in 2007, this burgeoning financial industry already involved more than four hundred banks and over a billion dollars in investments.[27] By the middle of the next decade, that figure is expected to more than double.[28] Yet this segment of the finance sector remains poorly understood, and even more poorly regulated.

The national security risk posed by *sharia* finance is essentially twofold. First, Western financial institutions generally have little familiarity with Islamic religious practices, and are forced to outsource verification and compliance to outside experts in Islamic law. Yet, without any fixed requirements on their credentials—and in the absence of rigorous vetting procedures—many of these advisors have ended up being prominent Islamist clerics. For example, Yusuf al-Qaradawi, one of the Muslim Brotherhood's leading ideologues, and prominent Pakistani Hanafi scholar Muhammad Taqi Usmani have been identified as two such high-paid—and radical—clerical consultants.[29] And all too often, when given the chance, these religious leaders are prone to carry radical religious ideas from the pulpit to the boardroom.

Second, and related, is the practice of *zakat* (alms). Under Islamic law, Muslims are required to give 2.5 percent of their earnings to charity, and the same rule applies for revenue generated from investments. In the abstract, such a requirement is benign, even beneficial. But since Muslim scholars have identified organizations that carry out *jihad* to be acceptable recipients of such alms,[30] there is a very real risk that the charitable donations so generated could provide material assistance to terrorist organizations.

This potentially sinister synergy has only been made more acute by the onset of the current global financial crisis. The U.S. federal government, scrambling to provide economic stability via increasing intervention in a troubled market, has begun following the lead of its counterparts in Europe, offering *sharia*-compliant financial vehicles as part of a push to attract financial backing from abroad. Thus, in November of 2008, the U.S. Treasury Department, working in conjunction with Harvard University's Islamic Finance Project, hosted a high-profile forum intended to explain and popularize *sharia*-compliant finance. Officially, its goal was fairly mundane: "to help inform the policy community about Islamic financial services."[31] But the event generated a massive outpouring of protest from a wide range of opponents, who warned that it constituted an implicit endorsement of the controversial financial practice on the part of the U.S. government.[32]

It would be tempting to view this event as a one-time occurrence. But the November 2008 scandal was both a legitimate manifestation of concern among national security practitioners and a portent of things to come. With *sharia* finance increasingly prevalent as a financial practice, the danger that money invested in such a manner can be siphoned off or redirected to terrorists is simply too great to be ignored. Rather than uncritically subsidizing and expanding this fledgling industry, the U.S. government needs to expend greater effort trying to regulate it. Better transparency protocols among leading investment banks on their *sharia*-compliant financial products, coupled with more stringent vetting of so-called "*sharia* advisors" (and the disqualification of those with clear linkages to radical Islamic groups), would do much to quell domestic fears of this new phenomenon—and to ensure that it does not emerge as a new source of financial support to our enemies.

EXPLOITING IRAN'S ECONOMIC VULNERABILITIES

Of all the potential financial targets in the current war, none are as vulnerable as the Islamic Republic of Iran. With oil production topping 4 million barrels a day and some 981 trillion cubic feet of proven natural gas reserves, Iran today may be a *bona fide* energy superpower.[33] But its inefficient, centrally planned economy—and the regime's array of latent economic vulnerabilities—make it an ideal target for coordinated financial pressure from the international community.

So far, Western nations have failed to grasp this fact. In the evolving debate over how to deal with Iran's radical regime, policymakers in Washington and European capitals alike have thrown their weight behind a range of strategies, from diplomatic engagement, to deterrence, to preemptive military action. Economic measures, however, have received comparatively short shrift in their calculus. That is because conventional wisdom has it that the United States and its allies possess little leverage that they can bring to bear against the Iranian regime and its terrorist network.

The conventional wisdom is wrong. Even the United States, despite its lack of trade relations with the Islamic Republic, has a considerable number of economic tools at its disposal. America's allies and trading partners, who, almost without exception, maintain extensive economic ties to Iran, possess far more. What has been missing so far has been a coordinated strategy to exploit the myriad chinks in Iran's economic armor.

The Achilles' heel of the Iranian regime, and the most attractive opening for Western strategy, lies at the intersection of two economic trends. The first is the Iranian regime's deep dependence on foreign supplies of gasoline. Despite its massive oil output, Iran still relies on refined petroleum from abroad for the steady functioning of its economy. The U.S. Department of Energy estimates that Iran is currently the world's second largest importer of gasoline, with foreign supplies accounting for approximately 40 percent of its total annual consumption.[34] The cause is an acute shortage of refining capacity, which has made Iran dependent on foreign sources to supply much of the four hundred thousand barrels of gasoline that are consumed daily by Iranian citizens.

The second is Iran's antiquated system of extensive economic subsidies. During the 1970s, as opposition to the Shah grew on the Iranian street, Islamic thinkers like Ali Shariati and Mahmoud Taleqani gravitated to a sort of socialized Shi'ism as an antidote to the Shah's "decadent" capitalist policies.[35] Khomeini was deeply influenced by their ideas; in his 1979 manifesto, *Islamic Government*, he extolled the virtues of governmental custodianship over the "collecting, safeguarding and spending [of] funds."[36] And when he swept to power in Tehran that year, Khomeini wasted no time putting these policies into practice. Three decades on, Iran's economy is still saddled with these socialist tendencies. According to the International Monetary Fund, roughly 27 percent of the country's entire annual gross domestic product is currently eaten up by costly federal subsidies.[37] Of these, the most conspicuous are in the energy realm, where the regime keeps prices at artificial rock-bottom rates as a gesture of goodwill toward its people. It does so at a staggering cost: perhaps as much as $45 billion annually.[38]

The combination of these two trends has made Iran uniquely vulnerable to measures that target its petroleum imports. Yet so far, neither the United States nor its allies have done anything serious to exploit this opening. During its time in office, the Bush administration shied away from measures that targeted Iran's petroleum imports, fearful of what Secretary of State Condoleezza Rice termed potential "bad effects on the Iranian people."[39] So did its opposition across the political aisle, albeit for very different reasons—worries that such economic pressure would be used simply as a prelude to war with Iran.[40] The resulting state of inertia has so far paralyzed America's willingness to push its allies to take advantage of a potentially fatal economic vulnerability.

Iranian policymakers, meanwhile, are acutely aware of this vulnerability and actively working to eliminate it. Over the past two years, the Iranian government has enacted a rationing plan establishing strict monthly quotas on gasoline for ordinary Iranians, and simultaneously attempted to institute steep cuts to its petrol purchases from abroad.[41] It has outlined an ambitious plan for upgrades to six of Iran's nine existing refineries and the construction of two new plants—moves cumulatively expected to boost the country's refining capabilities by nearly a million barrels daily by early next decade.[42] And, since taking office in August 2005, Iranian president Mahmoud Ahmadinejad has mapped out an extensive initiative to transition his country's energy sector from its current dependence on oil to vastly greater exploitation of natural gas by the middle of the next decade.[43]

Over time, these steps can be expected to significantly reduce Iran's vulnerability to external pressure on its energy sector. For the time being, however, the Iranian regime still faces what some have termed a "gasoline time bomb"[44]—a deep dependency on steady supplies of refined petroleum from abroad, and a fatal vulnerability to their elimination.

The West can exploit this opening by targeting the sources of Iran's petroleum habit—and systematically eliminating them. After all, these suppliers are well known; between March 2006 and March 2007 (Iranian calendar year 1385), the Iranian regime imported gasoline from sixteen countries—the United Arab Emirates (UAE), India, the Netherlands, France, Singapore, Turkmenistan, Azerbaijan, Sudan, Belarus, Turkey, Kuwait, Taiwan, Spain, Sweden, Saudi Arabia, and Bulgaria—at a price tag of some $4.2 billion.[45] So are the middlemen. Currently, just four companies—the Swiss firm Vitol, the Swiss/Dutch firm Trafigura, British Petroleum, and France's Total—sell Iran nearly all of its gasoline.[46]

If these countries and corporations were squeezed hard enough that they began to rethink participation in the Iran petroleum business, the effects on the Iranian economy would be enormous. Faced with even a partial gasoline embargo, the Iranian regime would be forced to deplete its hard currency reserves as it scrambles to secure new sources of refined petroleum. Such a cut-off could also cause serious work stoppages in "gasoline heavy" industrial sectors such as shipping, bringing commerce within the Islamic Republic to a standstill. And, if robust and sustained for long enough, such a blockade could impact the stability of the Iranian regime itself, prompting widespread unrest over rising petroleum prices, stricter rationing, or both.

All of which goes a long way toward explaining why a growing number of observers in Washington believe that, when it comes to applying economic pressure on Iran, a gasoline embargo could be a game-changer. "Given Iran's extraordinarily heavy dependence on imported gasoline," Orde Kittrie of the Foundation for the Defense of Democracies has written, "it may be our best remaining hope for peacefully convincing Iran to desist from developing nuclear weapons."[47]

While a gasoline embargo may be the best way to apply economic pressure to the Islamic Republic, it is hardly the only one. Another is to target Iran's "oligarchs," the small group of individuals and organizations that—much like their counterparts in Russia—today exert sweeping control over the Iranian economy.

Perhaps the most public of these is the extended family of former Iranian president (and current Assembly of Experts and Expediency Council head) Ali Akbar Hashemi Rafsanjani, which now virtually controls copper mining in Iran, the regime's lucrative pistachio trade, and a number of profitable industrial and export-import businesses.[48] Rafsanjani alone is believed to have amassed a personal fortune of close to $2 billion, largely by obtaining—and then failing to repay—loans from the country's state-owned banks.[49]

A related financial power center is Iran's *bonyads*, the sprawling, largely unregulated religious/social foundations that are overseen by Iran's supreme leader. Arguably the most important of these is the *Bonyad-e Mostazafan* (Foundation of the Oppressed), a complex network of an estimated 1,200 firms created in 1979 with seed money from the Shah's coffers.[50] Another is the *Bonyad-e Shahid*, a colossal conglomerate of industrial, agricultural, construction, and commercial companies with some 350 offices and tens of thousands of employees.[51] The sums controlled by these organs are enormous, estimated at more than 30 percent of Iran's national GDP (and as much as two-thirds of the country's non-oil GDP).[52]

Then there is the *Pasdaran*, or Iranian Revolutionary Guard Corps, Iran's feared clerical army. In recent years, the *Pasdaran* has emerged as a major economic force within the Islamic Republic, in command of numerous construction, industrial, transportation, and energy projects, as well as various commercial enterprises valued in the billions of dollars.[53] This power has been reinforced by preferential treatment from Iranian President Mahmoud Ahmadinejad. Himself a Guardsman, Ahmadinejad has funneled massive amounts of commercial business, and allotted preferential government posts, to his former comrades-in-arms. The result has been what some have termed a "creeping *coup d'etat*," in which Iran's clerical elite, long the economic center of gravity within the Islamic Republic, increasingly has been eclipsed by its own ideological muscle.[54]

This economic hierarchy provides an opening for targeted financial measures that restrict the ability of these individuals and organizations to access international markets—and curtail their capacity to engage in commerce. Over the years, the United States has made some inroads on that score. Since 2005, it has backed a series of international measures, orchestrated via the United Nations, to put pressure on the Iranian regime by imposing sanctions on key firms and individuals involved in Iran's WMD programs. In tandem with these efforts, the United States has begun to take a number of meaningful independent steps intended to put pressure on Iran's "super-empowered" economic actors. Far and away the most significant of these was the Bush administration's October 2007 designation of the *Pasdaran* as a "Specially Designated Global Terrorist" under U.S. law. The move was historic; it marked only the second time the U.S. government had blacklisted the armed forces of another nation. (The first took place during World War II, when the government of Franklin Delano Roosevelt explicitly targeted Hitler's Waffen SS). It was also potentially far-reaching; the designation provided the U.S. government with the authority to target the various companies and commercial entities controlled by the *Pasdaran*, and to systematically begin to exclude them from international markets.

These early steps should be compounded by additional ones, the goal of which would be to identify and isolate Iran's "super-empowered" economic actors. If applied swiftly and comprehensively, such measures could have a pronounced effect on regime decision making.

The United States also holds the power to exploit Iran's economic mismanagement. When a relative political unknown named Mahmoud Ahmadinejad unexpectedly won the Iranian presidency in the summer of 2005, it was a telling indicator of the depths of the economic malaise now gripping the Islamic Republic. During the election, Ahmadinejad's populist campaign, with its emphasis on rooting out corruption and providing economic dividends for ordinary Iranians, tapped into popular discontent with the lack of prosperity on the Iranian street. And, partially as a result, Ahmadinejad handily defeated his opponent, former president Ali Akbar Hashemi Rafsanjani.

But campaigning is one thing; governing quite another. Since coming to power, president Ahmadinejad's fiscal policies—ranging from profligate spending on social programs to arbitrary changes in the national banking rate—have been as erratic as they have been far-reaching, and the effects on the Iranian economy have been nothing short of ruinous. As of October 2008, Iranian central bank statistics put the national rate of inflation near 30 percent.[55] The price of domestic goods has likewise soared, with the cost of staples such as steak, rice, and beans rising nearly 50 percent during the month of September 2008 alone.[56]

These economic missteps have been dramatically exacerbated by the global economic meltdown. Early on, Iranian officials greeted news of mounting international financial turmoil with jubilation, celebrating what they saw as "divine punishment" for the West's aggression against the Muslim world.[57] It did not take long, however, for Iran itself to feel the pinch. Saddled with costly subsidies and heavily dependent on gasoline from abroad, Iran requires a far higher price per barrel for world oil than its neighbors in order to stay solvent. And the constriction of world markets, with the attendant sudden, steep drop in oil prices, has been nothing short of devastating for the Iranian regime's bottom line. According to International Monetary Fund estimates, oil prices must remain above $90 a barrel in order for Iran to turn a profit, and at $90 for the regime to "break even."[58] And with world oil prices substantially below that threshold, the Iranian regime has begun to devour itself from within, progressively depleting its hard currency reserves in order to stay afloat.

A growing number of observers have taken notice of this trend. "Iran is ripe for deflating," New York Times columnist Thomas Friedman has written. "Its power was inflated by the price of oil and the popularity of its leader, who was cheered simply because he was willing to poke America with a stick. But as a real nation-building enterprise, the Islamic Revolution in Iran has been an abject failure."[59]

Washington is in a position to accelerate this decline. If implemented in a coordinated fashion by the United States and its international partners, economic measures that exacerbate Iran's destabilizing internal conditions (by further raising the internal rate of inflation, prompting additional abrupt commodity price hikes, or sparking commercial shortages) have the ability to exploit the existing fissures between the Iranian regime and its people, and to galvanize far greater internal opposition to government practices.

Finally, it is possible for the United States to take a page from its Cold War playbook and marginalize Iran in the global market. During the decades of the Cold War, it was widely understood that the Soviet Union was operating an inefficient, decrepit, centrally planned economy. The reason it managed to stay in business was that the Soviet leadership was able to harness the country's vast natural resource wealth—in minerals, chemicals, and, most of all, oil—to build economic bridges to the West.

These contacts made the countries of Europe increasingly dependent on Soviet commodities, and allowed the USSR to stay in business despite its internal economic contradictions.

Thus, when the Reagan administration decided to wage economic warfare against the USSR, there was a clear "point of entry" for it to exploit. And the Reagan White House did just that, outlining—and then implementing—a qualitatively new economic policy that harnessed the Soviet Union's dependence on East-West trade as a way of preventing a Soviet arms buildup and reducing Moscow's opportunity to exercise leverage over the West. The results were unmistakable. As one historian has noted, "The Reagan administration began in early 1981 and by the time the president left office in 1989 the Soviet Bloc was already in the early stages of its final dissolution, bringing with it the collapse of the Soviet Union itself and the end of the Cold War." [60]

Today, the United States can employ much the same strategy toward Iran. With its oil-heavy economy and inefficient central planning practices, Iran is heavily dependent on trade with the outside world—and deeply vulnerable to the disruption of this commerce.

To its credit, the United States has begun to exploit this opening. Since early 2006, the Treasury Department has spearheaded a broad-based effort to systematically squeeze Iran's capacity to engage in international commerce. This offensive has included cutting off at least four of Iran's leading banks—Bank Saderat, Bank Sepah, Bank Melli, and the Export Development Bank of Iran—from the U.S. financial system, as well as diplomatic and political outreach intended to chill investor confidence in the Islamic Republic. [61]

These efforts, compounded and amplified by Security Council measures against Iran, have succeeded in mobilizing an international campaign to impose financial costs on Iran for its rogue behavior. And foreign financial institutions have responded; when tallied in October 2008, some eighty banks were estimated to have curtailed their business dealings with Iran. [62] Iranian officials, meanwhile, have become increasingly nervous. "We had embarked on a serious and breathtaking game of chess with America's Treasury Department," Iran's then-finance minister, Davoud Danesh Jaffari, is reported to have warned his staff in April 2008 before leaving office. [63]

Much more can be done. U.S. authorities can start by directly targeting Iran's Central Bank, known as Bank Markazi. Such a measure is admittedly unusual; historically, the United States has been loathe to target foreign central banks, seeing these entities—which regulate currency, set interbank lending rates, and manage national inflation—as a staple of smooth international commerce. But Bank Markazi operates as much more than simply a market mechanism. Since the start of international sanctions against Iran some six years ago, it has played an instrumental role in helping Iranian financial entities skirt Western pressure. Bank Markazi governor Tahmasb Mazaheri admitted as much when he told a London conference in February 2008 that "[t]he central bank assists Iranian private and state-owned banks to do their commitments regardless of the pressure on them."[64] By doing so, it has violated U.S. laws that make institutions that aid sanctioned entities punishable themselves, making it a legitimate, and inviting, target.

Another target of opportunity is those companies that continue to carry out commerce with Iran. When it passed the Iran-Libya Sanctions Act (ILSA) in 1996, Congress had a clear goal in mind: to curb Tehran's capacity to acquire weapons of mass destruction and support international terrorism by forcing foreign companies and governments to scale back their economic involvement with the Iranian regime.[65] Over the past decade, however, this commitment has been honored entirely in the breach. Successive U.S. governments—irrespective of political affiliation—have consistently prioritized bilateral trade over international security, waiving application of ILSA and other relevant laws aimed at penalizing Iran for its rogue behavior.

This constitutes a major miscalculation. Such "second tier" sanctions are a critical tool in the West's economic arsenal vis-à-vis Iran. Simply put, continued commerce with an increasingly intransigent Iranian regime cannot continue to be perceived as "cost free" by the international community. By enacting—and then *actively enforcing*—such measures, policymakers in Washington have the ability to force Iran's trading partners to choose between doing business with Iran and conducting commerce with the United States, and to provide them with the political rationale necessary to make the proper choice.

CRISIS AND OPPORTUNITY

All politics are local, the saying goes, and the current state of the U.S. economic warfare effort is a testament to this fact. Today, applying real financial pressure against our terrorist adversaries appears to be the farthest thing from the minds of policymakers in Washington. Since its onset in the late summer of 2008, the global financial crisis has presented the United States with its greatest financial challenge since the Great Depression. Regulators and lawmakers are now scrambling to come up with solutions to failing corporations, toxic mortgage debt, and dangerous derivatives. In the process, serious efforts to move the goalposts on the financial front of our current struggle seem to have fallen by the wayside.

Yet the economic crisis that has engulfed the international system since the fall of 2008 has brought with it both serious danger and unexpected opportunity. For, however bad the economic crisis might be for the United States, others are weathering it far worse.

There is no shortage of indicators that this is the case. In Iran, plummeting oil prices have presented the regime with a serious economic crisis, one that Iran's ayatollahs may well not be able to weather intact without foreign assistance.[66] Still others, from Russia to Saudi Arabia to China, though more fiscally stable, are experiencing a far steeper economic decline—and a more profound financial pinch—than we in the West.[67] And while al-Qaeda's reliance on the informal economy has made it more resilient than most to the ups and downs of a turbulent global market,[68] there is reason to believe that a tightening of purse strings abroad, coupled with continued international cooperation on terrorism financing, will continue to chip away at the bin Laden network's financial capabilities in the years ahead.[69] All of which gives credence to the wry observation of *Wall Street Journal* columnist Brett Stephens that, "when the tide laps at Gulliver's waistline, it usually means the Lilliputians are already 10 feet under."[70]

The global economic meltdown, in other words, is not simply a crisis. It is also an opening for the United States to take the economic offensive in its struggle against the forces of radical Islam and those states and entities that sustain them. With its economic clout, America has the ability to enact measures that would make it more difficult for terrorists and their sponsors to access the international system, to impose real costs on those that facilitate their movement in the global economy, and to compete with them on a grassroots level. In order to do that, however, Washington must be bold enough to seize the economic moment.

NOTES

1. Peter Grier, "Frozen Assets: US has Crimped Al Qaeda Funds," *Christian Science Monitor*, October 30, 2007, http://www.csmonitor.com/2007/1030/p01s07-usgn.htm.

2. Michael Jacobson, "Grading U.S. Performance against Terrorism Financing," Washington Institute For Near East Policy *Policywatch* 1280, September 5, 2007, http://www.washingtoninstitute.org/print.php?template=C05&CID=2656.

3. *The 9/11 Commission Report: Final Report of the National Commission on Terrorist Attacks Upon the United States* (New York: W.W. Norton, 2004), 169.

4. In his memoir, financier Bernard Baruch details how the War Industries Board, which President Woodrow Wilson established in 1917 and on which Baruch served as chairman, presided over a "drastic redirection of the nation's resources" that allowed the nation to persevere in the First World War. Bernard M. Baruch, *Baruch: The Public Years* (New York: Holt, Rinehart and Winston, 1960), 53–74.

5. As cited in Gordon Lubold, "Few Americans Share Iraq War's Sacrifices," *Christian Science Monitor*, March 26, 2007, http://www.csmonitor.com/2007/0326/p01s01-ussc.html?page=1.

6. Letter from Acting SEC Chairman Laura Unger to Rep. Frank Wolf, May 8, 2001, as cited in Edward F. Greene et al., *U.S. Regulation of the International Securities and Derivatives Markets*,8th ed. (Aspen, Colorado: Aspen Publishers, 2005), 8–93.

7. Press Release, Office of Senator Chris Dodd, "Chairman Dodd Sends Letter to SEC: Calls for Greater Disclosure on Investments in Iran, Sudan," May 31, 2007, http://dodd.senate.gov/index.php?q=node/3923.

8. Conflict Securities Advisory Group, "What Is Global Security Risk?" February 1, 2009, http://www.conflictsecurities.com/security/index.cfm.

9. "Lukoil Bemoans Iran Sanctions," *Russia Today*, October 22, 2007, http://www.russiatoday.com/business/news/15877.

10. One such group is the Washington-based Conflict Securities Advisory Group, which has created a proprietary database to help investors research and identify companies doing business with state sponsors of terror.

11. Roger W. Robinson, testimony before the House of Representatives Foreign Affairs Committee Subcommittee on International Monetary Policy, Trade and Technology and Subcommittee on Terrorism, Nonproliferation and Trade, April 18, 2007, http://www.globalsecurity.org/security/library/congress/2007_h/070418-robinson.htm.

12. Frank Gaffney, testimony before the House of Representatives Foreign Affairs Committee Subcommittee on Terrorism, Nonproliferation and Trade,

May 24, 2007, http://www.centerforsecuritypolicy.org/Modules/NewsManager/ShowSectionNews.aspx?CategoryID=140&SubCategoryID=150&NewsID=13988.

13. In its second term, the Bush administration made no secret of its displeasure with the progress made by various divestment initiatives on the state and local level during its tenure. And, operating by proxy, it largely succeeded in stymieing congressional efforts to give these state laws greater potency. See, for example, Shmuel Rosner, "Bush Administration Opposes Bills on Divestment from Iran, Sudan," *Ha'aretz* (Tel Aviv), August 29, 2007; Author's conversations with Congressional staff, Washington, DC, October 2007.

14. See, for example, Senator Barack Obama, address to the American Israel Public Affairs Committee, Washington, DC, June 3, 2008, http://www.npr.org/templates/story/story.php?storyId=91150432.

15. See, for example, Esther Pan, "Lebanon: Election Results," Council on Foreign Relations *Backgrounder*, June 20, 2005, http://www.cfr.org/publication/8195/lebanon.html.

16. See, for example, Gal Luft, "Hizballahland," *Commentary* 116, no. 1 (2003): 56–57.

17. As cited in Stephen Ulph, "Al-Zawahiri Takes Hamas to Task," Jamestown Foundation *Terrorism Monitor* 3, no. 9 (2006), http://www.jamestown.org/terrorism/news/article.php?articleid=2369916.

18. See, for example, Elie Krakowski, "How to Win the Peace in Afghanistan," *Weekly Standard* 007, no. 41 (2002), http://www.weeklystandard.com/content/public/articles/000/000/001/403lrkrt.asp?pg=1.

19. Rebecca Davis O'Brien, "Intelligence Report: Who Gets U.S. Foreign Aid," *PARADE*, December 14, 2008, http://www.parade.com/news/intelligence-report/archive/who-gets-us-foreign-aid.html.

20. United States Office of Management and Budget, "Pakistan: All Spigots," n.d. (author's collection).

21. Yuval Levin, "American Aid to the Middle East: A Tragedy of Good Intentions," Institute for Advanced Strategic and Political Studies *Research Papers in Strategy* 11, December 2000, http://www.iasps.org/strat11/strategic11.pdf.

22. Vernon Ruttan, *United States Development Assistance Policy* (Baltimore: Johns Hopkins University Press, 1996), 256.

23. John F. Kennedy, *Collected Presidential Papers, 1963* (Washington: Government Printing Office, 1963), 317, as cited in Levin, "American Aid to the Middle East: A Tragedy of Good Intentions."

24. R. James Woolsey, "The Long War Of The 21st Century," in Barry R. Schneider and Jim A Davis, eds. *The War Next Time: Countering Rogue States and Terrorists Armed with Chemical and Biological Weapons* (Maxwell Air Force Base: USAF Counterproliferation Center, 2004).

25. Author's conversations with senior U.S. economic official, Washington, DC, December 2008 and January 2009.

26. See, for example, "Gersten Savage Chairs Conference on Islamic Finance in North America," PR Newswire, October 11, 2007, http://www.prnewswire .com/cgi-bin/stories.pl?ACCT=ind_focus.story&STORY=/www/story/10-11 -2007/0004680502&EDATE=THU+Oct+11+2007,+03:43+PM.

27. Alex Alexiev, "Islamic Finance or Financing Islamism?" familysecurity matters.org, October 24, 2007, http://www.familysecuritymatters.org/index .php?id=1385092.

28. Ibid.

29. Alex R. Alexiev, "Jihad Comes to Wall Street," National Review Online, April 3, 2008, http://article.nationalreview.com/q=ZjBhMTM5MTlmN2YzNzE 0MmFkOTg2OGYxNWM2MGNiNTQ.

30. Jonathan D. Halevi, "What Drives Saudi Arabia to Persist in Terrorist Financing?" Jerusalem Center for Public Affairs Briefing no. 531, June 1, 2005, http://www.jcpa.org/jl/vp531.htm.

31. Seminar announcement, "Islamic Finance 101," U.S. Department of the Treasury and the Islamic Finance Project—Harvard University, November 8, 2008, http://www.saneworks.us/uploads/news/applications/7.pdf.

32. See, for example, Chelsea Schilling, "U.S. Treasury Teaches 'Islamic Finance 101,'" worldnetdaily.com, November 5, 2008, http://www.worldnetdaily .com/index.php?fa=PAGE.view&pageId=80003.

33. Statistics derived from Department of Energy, Energy Information Administration, "Iran Energy Profile," n.d., http://tonto.eia.doe.gov/country/ country_time_series.cfm?fips=IR, and British Petroleum, BP Statistical Review of World Energy, June 2008, http://www.bp.com/liveassets/bp_internet/globalbp/ globalbp_uk_english/reports_and_publications/statistical_energy_review _2008/STAGING/local_assets/downloads/pdf/statistical_review_of_world _energy_full_review_2008.pdf

34. U.S. Department of Energy, Energy Information Administration, "Country Analysis Brief: Iran," October 2007, http://www.eia.doe.gov/emeu/cabs/ Iran/Oil.html.

35. Vali Nasr, The Shia Revival: How Conflicts within Islam will Shape the Future (New York: W.W. Norton, 2007), 126–30.

36. Ruhollah Khomeini, Islamic Government (New York: Manor Books, 1979), 22.

37. International Monetary Fund, "Islamic Republic of Iran: Selected Issues," August 2008, http://www.imf.org/external/pubs/ft/scr/2008/cr08285.pdf.

38. "Gov't to Seek Extra $7 Bln to Import Fuel," Fars (Tehran), October 1, 2008, http://english.farsnews.com/newstext.php?nn=8707100349; "Iran Inflation Keeps Pressure On Ahmadinejad," Reuters, March 24, 2008, http:// uk.reuters.com/article/worldNews/idUKL2037673520080324?sp=true.

39. As cited in Bret Stephens, "Secretary of Turbulence," *Wall Street Journal*, September 30, 2006, http://www.opinionjournal.com/editorial/feature.html?id=110009020.

40. "Democrats Quietly Defeat Resolution Authorizing Iran Blockade," world tribune.com, October 21, 2008, http://www.worldtribune.com/worldtribune/WTARC/2008/ss_iran0628_10_21.asp.

41. "Iran Cuts Petrol Imports to Save Nearly $3 Bln," Fars (Tehran), September 26, 2007.

42. Department of Energy, "Country Analysis Brief: Iran."

43. This effort reportedly includes 1) converting most existing vehicles in Iran to run on natural gas over a five-year period; 2) rapidly phasing out old, inefficient vehicles; 3) making all new vehicles in the Islamic Republic "flex fuel" (able to operate on both oil and natural gas), and; 4) expanding the nation's network of filling stations to make them capable of selling both oil and natural gas. See Anne Korin and Gal Luft, "Ahmadinejad's Gas Revolution: A Plan to Defeat Economic Sanctions," Institute for the Analysis of Global Security, December 2006, http://www.iags.org/iran121206.pdf.

44. "Iran Faces a Gasoline Time Bomb," *Petroleum Intelligence Weekly* 45, no. 38 (2006): 4.

45. "Iran Imported Gasoline from 16 States in 2006," Mehr (Tehran), May 20, 2007. (author's collection)

46. A fifth, India's Reliance Industries, announced in January 2009 that it was ceasing gasoline supplies to Iran after a group of lawmakers put pressure on the U.S. Export-Import Bank to cut off loan guarantees to the firm unless it did so. See Nevin John, "RIL Gives in to US Pressure, Stops Gasoline to Iran," *Business Standard* (New Delhi), January 7, 2009, http://www.business-standard.com/india/news/ril-gives-in-to-us-pressure-stops-gasoline-to-iran/00/26/345499/.

47. Orde F. Kittrie, "How to Put the Squeeze on Iran," *Wall Street Journal*, November 13, 2008, http://online.wsj.com/article/SB122654026060023113.html?mod=djemEditorialPage.

48. Paul Klebnikov, "Millionaire Mullahs." forbes.com, July 21, 2003, http://www.forbes.com/forbes/2003/0721/056.html.

49. See, for example, "Mr. R's Misconduct," Baztab (Tehran), October 16, 2006.

50. Robert D. Kaplan, "A Bazaari's World," *The Atlantic Monthly* 277, no. 3 (1996): 28.

51. Wilfried Buchta, *Who Rules Iran? The Structure of Power in the Islamic Republic* (Washington, DC: Washington Institute for Near East Policy and Konrad Adenauer Stiftung, 2000), 75.

52. Ibid.; See also Kenneth Katzman, Statement before the Joint Economic Committee of the United States Congress, July 25, 2006.

53. Mehdi Khalaji, "Iran's Revolutionary Guard Corps, Inc.," Washington Institute for Near East Policy *Policywatch* no. 1273, August 17, 2007, http://www .washingtoninstitute.org/templateC05.php?CID=2649.

54. Amir Taheri, "The Odd Guard," *New York Post*, August 29, 2007, http:// www.nypost.com/seven/08292007/postopinion/opedcolumnists/the_odd _guard.htm.

55. "Iran Inflation Nears 30 Percent in September—Media," Reuters, October 9, 2008, http://www.reuters.com/article/marketsNews/ idUSDAH92588020081009.

56. "Food Prices in Iran Soar 50pc in September," Agence France Presse, September 29, 2008, http://www.thepeninsulaqatar.com/Display_news .asp?section=World_News&subsection=Gulf%2C+Middle+East+%26+Africa&m onth=September2008&file=World_News2008092914949.xml.

57. Ayatollah Ahmad Jannati, as cited in Middle East Media Research Institute *Special Dispatch* no. 2070, October 3, 2008, http://www.memri.org/bin/articles.cgi?Page=countries&Area=iran&ID=SP207008.

58. "Saudi Needs Oil Above $49 to Avoid Deficit; Qatar Break-Even $24: IMF," *Gulf Times* (Doha), September 21, 2008, http://www.gulf-times .com/site/topics/article.asp?cu_no=2&item_no=242775&version=1&template _id=48&parent_id=28.

59. Thomas L. Friedman, "Sleepless in Tehran," *New York Times*, October 28, 2008, http://www.nytimes.com/2008/10/29/opinion/29friedman.html?_r= 1&ref=opinion&oref=login.

60. See Norman A. Bailey, *The Strategic Plan That Won The Cold War: National Security Decision Directive 75* (McLean, VA: Potomac Foundation, 1998).

61. For a good overview of this effort, see Robin Wright, "Stuart Levey's War," *New York Times Magazine*, November 2, 2008, 28–33.

62. Ibid.

63. Ibid.

64. As cited in Glenn R. Simpson, "U.S. Weighs Sanctions on Iran's Central Bank," *Wall Street Journal*, February 26, 2008, A1.

65. *Iran and Libya Sanctions Act of 1996*, Public Law 104-172, August 5, 1996.

66. See Ilan Berman, "Iran's Economic Dire Straits," forbes.com, November 19, 2008, http://www.forbes.com/2008/11/19/iran-economy-oil-oped-cx_ib _1119berman_print.html.

67. Brett Stephens, "America Will Remain the Superpower," *Wall Street Journal*, October 14, 2008, http://online.wsj.com/article/SB122394103108030821 .html.

68. Sebastian Abbot, "Analysts: Al-Qaida has Funds despite Economic Woes," Associated Press, October 16, 2008, http://abcnews.go.com/International/ wireStory?id=6050568.

69. Matthew Levitt and Michael Jacobson, "The U.S. Campaign to Squeeze Terrorists' Financing," *Columbia Journal of International Affairs* 62, no. 1 (2008): 67–85.

70. Stephens, "America Will Remain the Superpower."

5

WEAPONIZING
INTERNATIONAL LAW

Today, it has become something of a common refrain that the West has suddenly found itself in a qualitatively different kind of conflict. Politicians of all political stripes have warned that America is now fighting a "new kind of war" than the type that predominated during the twentieth century.

But what exactly does this mean, on a practical level? The years since the attacks of September 11 have made clear that our current adversaries are motivated by very different things than were their predecessors. As former CIA director R. James Woolsey has pointed out, the leaders of the Soviet Union may have been radical, but they were rational; they did not believe in the next life, and so they wanted to live well in this one.[1] This meant that, as a practical matter, it was possible to establish some semblance of normal relations with the Kremlin, even at the height of the Cold War. Moscow's leaders, quite simply, understood the necessity for coexistence on an economic and diplomatic level, even if they saw Soviet communism and Western capitalism as inherently in conflict with one another.

Not so now. Whether Sunni or Shi'a, Islamic radicals have gravitated to the view that their conflict with the United States and its allies is an existential one, in which no quarter can be given or compromise reached. A half-century ago, Islamic thinkers like Sayyid Qutb were already preaching about the "grand alliance of evil" represented by the West, and advocating the necessity of its violent overthrow.[2] Today, Osama bin Laden and his terrorist network have taken up this call, advocating the destruction of what they have called the "Zionist-Crusader alliance." And they are not alone. Iranian president Mahmoud Ahmadinejad, for example, has made no secret of his belief that "a historic war between the oppressor [Christians] and the world of Islam" is underway, and that his country is on the front lines of this struggle.[3]

In this conflict, the United States has found itself at a distinct disadvantage. America is certainly no stranger to warfare against asymmetric adversaries. "Since its independence, the U.S. has fought counterinsurgency campaigns against the Native Americans, against the South during the Civil War, in the Philippines, and, of course, in Vietnam," military scholars William Wunderle and Gabriel Lajeunesse write.[4] But it has tended to do so under a defined set of political and legal parameters—many of which have little or no relevance to our current adversaries and their conflict with us.

NAVIGATING THE NEW WAY OF WAR

In order to fully appreciate why the United States is so ill-suited for today's conflict, it is necessary to understand the principles that underpin the way the West operates in peace and war.

The first has to do with the preeminence of the nation-state. In the first part of the seventeenth century, Europe was in turmoil, wracked by religious strife between Protestants and Catholics that came to be known as the Thirty Years' War. When that conflict formally ended in 1648 with the Treaty of Westphalia, it ushered in a new political epoch on the Old Continent. More than three and a half centuries later, we still live in a "Westphalian" world—one in which the principal unit of measure is the nation-state. Thus the United Nations Charter, the closest thing international law has to a "constitution," concerns itself exclusively with governing conduct among nations. Likewise, only states can become signatories to the Hague and Geneva Conventions, the essential building blocks of the modern laws of war.

This does not mean that non-state actors have no legal standing at all. Since the late 1960s, more and more agreements have begun to recognize that at least some non-state actors do matter, in an international sense. Overwhelmingly, however, the international system is still "state-centric" in nature—concerned with how countries relate to one another, how they interact, and how they fight.

Second, and closely related to the idea of state power, is the concept of *pacta sunt servanda*. This principle, also enshrined in the Treaty of Westphalia, obligates Western nations to abide by those international agreements that they enter into. This simple notion—that agreements signed abroad must carry real legal force at home—serves as the touchstone for all of Western lawmaking and strategy. In the United States, this idea is embedded in the Constitution itself, which mandates that "all Treaties made, or which shall be made, under the Authority of the United States, shall be the supreme Law of the Land; and the Judges in every State shall be bound thereby, any Thing in the Constitution or Laws of any State to the Contrary notwithstanding."[5]

The third essential element of the Western political order is a status quo view of the international system. Good fences make good neighbors, the saying goes, and modern politics is overwhelmingly concerned with preserving the status quo in foreign affairs. The UN Charter, for example, formally outlaws war, obliging its members to "refrain in their international relations from the threat or use of force against the territorial integrity or political independence of any state."[6] The intention is clear; to prevent an outbreak of hostilities that could result in a drastic alteration of the current balance of power between the nations of the world. This goal, perhaps more than any other, has become the organizing principle of modern Western politics, spawning countless multilateral institutions, transnational cooperation initiatives, and diplomatic efforts aimed at a preservation of the global peace.

Finally, Western powers by and large embrace a doctrine of "just war" that dictates and defines when, and how, they fight. This tradition has its roots in antiquity; in the fourth century, St. Augustine articulated the first principles of "just war theory" when he emphasized that, in order for killing to be just, it had to be carried out in a public (rather than private) capacity, and even then only if there was a clear threat to law and order. These early thoughts were expanded upon by later scholars. In the thirteenth century, the Dominican priest Thomas Aquinas identified three requirements for just war: the authority of a sovereign, a just cause, and a rightful intention (to advance good and avoid evil).[7] Two centuries after that, the philosopher and theologian Francisco de Vittoria (1492–1546) elaborated considerably on these tenets, declaring, among other things, that "the deliberate slaughter of innocents" was never "lawful in itself."[8]

So it went, throughout the centuries, as scholar upon scholar added layers of complexity to the doctrine of when and how conflicts should properly be fought. By the time Hugo Grotius, the father of modern international law, wrote his seminal treatise *De Jure Belli Ac Pacis* (On the Law of War and Peace) in 1625, the principles of just war had become well defined. In order to be deemed "just," Grotius and other scholars believed, warfare:

- needed to be authorized by legitimate authorities;
- could only be resorted to after a specific fault had taken place, and then only to make reparation for injury or restore what had been unjustly taken;
- had to advance good and avoid evil;
- except in cases of self defense, required a reasonable prospect of victory;
- could only be undertaken as a means of last resort;
- had to keep the innocent immune from attack during the fighting; and
- did not involve the use of disproportionate force.

These tenets remain relevant today, codified in international agreements such as the Hague and Geneva Conventions, which cumulatively provide the foundation of modern warfare: the *jus ad bellum* (justifications for going to war) and the *jus in bello* (conduct during wartime).

The way of war embraced by the West's Islamist adversaries, by contrast, could not be more different.

Al-Qaeda and its ideological fellow travelers, for example, reject outright the legitimacy of modern international law and politics built around the Westphalian system. Instead, they believe, as Allah Bukhsh K. Brohi made clear in his introduction to S. K. Malik's famous treatise on *The Quranic Concept of War*, that "no nation is sovereign since God alone is the only sovereign in Whom authority vests."[9] At best, therefore, the Westphalian system is seen as irrelevant to their interpretation of God's law; at worst, it is an unacceptable abrogation of it.

These radicals, therefore, reject completely the idea of secular governance embodied by the nation-state in favor of two very different units of measure. The first is the individual Muslim, whom radical scholars like Mohammed Abdel Salam Faraj have tasked with a personal responsibility for helping to spread Islam and taking up arms for it.[10] The second is the *umma*, the righteous community of believers that the Prophet Muhammad declared was owed greater allegiance than any clan, tribe, or nationality.[11]

The overriding objective of both is to expatriate disbelief. In the *jihadist* conception, the world is divided into two poles. The first is known as the *Dar al-Islam* (or house of submission), made up of pious Muslims who understand the supremacy of Islam and abide by the teachings of Allah. The second, the *Dar al-Harb* or house of war, is the part of the world that still does not submit to Allah's will, and is therefore seen as being actively "engaged in perpetuating defiance of the . . . Lord."[12] And the cardinal duty is to expand the former and diminish the latter—through active proselytization (*da'wa*) if possible, and by force of arms (*jihad*) if necessary.

Naturally, al-Qaeda also rejects any constraints on how it wages warfare. "The division of people into military or civilian is not part of Islamic law," al-Qaeda's chief strategist, Muhammad Khalil al-Hakaymah, has written. "Islamic law divides people into combatants and noncombatants. A combatant by the standard of Islamic law is anyone who himself fights or who helps the combat by his wealth or opinion."[13] And any weapon can be used to fight these foes. "There is no doubt that Allah has ordered us to target the unbelievers, to kill them and to fight them, by any means that can achieve this goal," the bin Laden network's top lieutenant in Iraq, Abu Musab al-Zarqawi, declared back in May 2005.[14] This has translated into an active pursuit of chemical, biological, and even nuclear weapons on the part of al-Qaeda, based on Osama bin Laden's conviction (articulated in his 1998 communiqué entitled "The Nuclear Bomb of Islam") that "it is the duty of the Muslims to prepare as much force as possible to terrorize the enemies of God."[15]

Shi'a radicals, for their part, generally assume a more nuanced stance. As a result of a confluence of religious and historical factors, Shi'ites throughout the Islamic world have grown to embrace the need for involvement in local politics. Thus, Iran today operates as a full-fledged member of the global community, party to numerous multilateral institutions and a signatory to a range of international agreements. Yet, thirty years after its Revolution, it still remains very much a radical, revolutionary state—one whose constitution commits it to the "struggle to extend the supremacy of God's Law in the world."[16] And its proxies function in much the same way. Hezbollah may be an integral part of the Lebanese political system, as well as the major provider of social services in the country's south, but its officials remain committed to the obliteration of Israel, and view America's destruction as a "policy, a strategy and a vision."[17]

SLOUCHING TOWARD A NEW STRATEGY

As the foregoing suggests, the struggle against radical Islam is fundamentally different from the types of conflicts that predominated during the nineteenth and twentieth centuries, when the corpus of rules and regulations that make up modern international law took root. Today's fight has little to do with conventional conflicts between great powers, and everything to do with transnational actors and rogue regimes. These new adversaries, unlike our old ones, more often than not do not adhere to the conventional "rules of the road" in the international system. And America desperately needs new laws and regulations for managing today's conflict, even as it protects and preserves the old ones that govern the way it interacts with the rest of the world.

Over the years, the United States has struggled to strike this balance. In the days after September 11, the Bush administration correctly recognized that the attacks on Washington and New York were tantamount to a declaration of war against the United States by the forces of radical Islam. In response, it launched a far-reaching effort to refashion what some have called "the law of September 10" to better confront the contemporary threat posed by al-Qaeda and other Islamic radicals.[18] But the way it went about doing so engendered no small measure of controversy, both at home and abroad.

Thus, President Bush's November 2001 executive order mandating that terrorists captured on the field of battle be tried in military tribunals, rather than conventional courts,[19] may have been built on the recognition that al-Qaeda was not a signatory to the Geneva Conventions and had explicitly rejected the established customs of war. But it raised concerns among civil libertarians about a potential lack of due process protections for those captured. So did the White House's vague definition of the "War on Terror" as an open-ended conflict, which led many to fear that al-Qaeda and Taliban "enemy combatants" could be held in U.S. custody indefinitely. Meanwhile, the network of secret prisons it erected for this purpose, as well the harsh interrogation measures used in them (such as "waterboarding"), opened the Bush administration up to charges from liberals and conservatives alike that it was engaging in torture—or, at the very least, that it was condoning practices that skirted perilously close to it.

The summer of 2006 marked a turning point of sorts in this tug-of-war. That June, the Supreme Court waded squarely into the evolving debate over law and the "War on Terror" when it ruled that Salim Ahmed Hamdan, a Yemeni national who had served as Osama bin Laden's personal driver and bodyguard before being captured in Afghanistan in 2001, could not be tried before a military tribunal because the process lacked sufficient protections under the laws of war.[20] The decision was a resounding indictment of the dominant view that held sway within the Bush administration: that the contemporary enemy—by virtue of its objectives as well as its tactics—operated well outside the protections of Geneva. Never mind that legally, the White House was on solid ground, since Hamdan had belonged to an organization that was not—indeed, could not be—a signatory to the Geneva Conventions, and that his treatment was on a par with that of other individuals in previous conflicts who had violated the laws and customs of war.[21]

In its aftermath, the Bush administration reversed course, agreeing to provide all prisoners in U.S. custody with Geneva Conventions protections.[22] But the damage was already done. The years that followed saw its legal policies increasingly discredited, politicized, and marginalized, with little thought given by either the pundits or the public to the underlying reason the Bush administration felt it necessary to institute those measures in the first place.

The current administration has gone in the opposite direction. Since taking office, President Barack Obama has made a rollback of Bush-era legal policies a top priority. As one of his first acts in office, he ordered the closure of the Camp X-Ray naval base in Guantanamo Bay, Cuba and other terrorist detention facilities, as well as the end of "coercive interrogations" of the prisoners held there.[23] These steps have been echoed by officials in his administration, who have recommended still more restrictions on the way the United States gathers information from suspected terrorists.[24] In other words, the Obama administration's approach has been defined in large measure by what it *will not do* in the course of prosecuting the current conflict. At least so far, it has failed to articulate a positive agenda for shaping the international legal system in a way that facilitates our fight. It will need to do so in short order, on two critical fronts.

TOWARD A STANDARD DEFINITION OF TERRORISM

One man's terrorist is another man's freedom fighter. Over the years, that refrain has been repeated so often in university classrooms and the musings of foreign policy cognoscenti that it has practically become conventional wisdom. As a matter of international law, however, it is completely false.

True, the United Nations currently has no standard definition for terrorism. While al-Qaeda is commonly understood to be a terrorist organization—and is treated as such in a range of UN resolutions and by a number of UN bodies—the classification of other Islamic radicals has proven to be much more controversial. Reaching consensus on the status of groups such as Hezbollah and Hamas has been particularly difficult, in no small measure because of the politics involved. Simply put, the Arab and Muslim worlds have historically equated violence against the state of Israel, however indiscriminate, with "resistance" rather than terror. The result has been deadlock over exactly who is, and who isn't, a terrorist in international terms.

But that does not mean that a workable, standardized definition does not exist. In fact, one does. It can be found embedded in the criteria for lawful combatancy enumerated in the laws of war.

These benchmarks are not new. For almost as long as armed warfare has existed, politicians and jurists have attempted to regulate it. During the Middle Ages, advocates of "just war" were already stipulating that war could only be waged if it was authorized by legitimate authorities. Over the centuries, subsequent formulations—codified by governments and followed by militaries and international organizations alike—strengthened and expanded the definition of who could, and who could not, legitimately participate in combat.

The goal was practical. After all, the narrower the definition of "legitimate" combatancy, the fewer participants there would be on the battlefield. A smaller war, in turn, would be more manageable and easier to end. By the early twentieth century, such considerations had been codified via the Hague Conventions into a clear four-part standard. In order to be considered a legitimate combatant, those engaged in hostilities were required to follow a defined chain of command, wear an emblem or insignia visible at a distance, carry their arms openly, and obey the laws of war during fighting (most directly by avoiding the targeting of civilians).

It is hard not to notice how conspicuously short of that standard our current adversaries actually fall. "Global jihadist networks," Andrew McCarthy, one of America's most astute legal scholars, explains, turn the system of civilized warfare enshrined in the Geneva Conventions "on its head." "Their modus operandi is to endanger civilians, directly by mass-destruction attacks and indirectly by blending into the population, complicating reprisals."[25] And by doing so, these groups explicitly reject even the minimum standards that would grant them some semblance of international legitimacy on the battlefield.

Others, however, do not. Self-determination movements, for example, have historically commanded significant global credibility. Thus the UN Charter, formulated in the aftermath of World War II and the end of the colonial era in the Middle East and North Africa, commits the international community to protecting the "equal rights and self-determination of peoples."[26] Over the years, in a variety of places (such as Kosovo and Taiwan), these tendencies have been encouraged and supported—provided the movements in question abide by a number of legal benchmarks. The message is clear: if you want to be a government, you have to act like one. And that includes honoring the tenets of civilized warfare, from respecting proportionality on the battlefield to sparing civilians from harm.

This contrast suggests that it is possible to create, and then to implement, a new operational definition of terrorism—one that focuses not on who terrorists are, but how they fight. To be sure, such a classification would matter little to al-Qaeda and its affiliated groups, which have already made clear their rejection of any constraints on warfare. But others, such as the Tamil Tigers of Sri Lanka or separatists in Chechnya, may choose to adapt their tactics as a way of gaining political relevance or garnering greater international credibility.

The precedent certainly exists. Not that long ago, even the world's most powerful Shi'a militia temporarily altered its *modus operandi* in order to garner greater global legitimacy. In the wake of Israel's May 2000 withdrawal from Lebanon, Hezbollah made a major bid for political power in Beirut. As part of that effort, the organization underwent a shift in military focus, turning its attention overwhelmingly to military—rather than civilian—targets.[27] None of this, of course, signaled a lasting change in Hezbollah's ideology, or in its long-term objectives. But its brief dalliance with international legitimacy suggests that, while it might be impossible to change the objectives of terrorist groups, it is possible to change the ways in which they seek to attain them.

The Bush administration, in its day, failed to take advantage of this opportunity. Its officials asserted, with merit, "that terrorists picked up off the battlefield—who don't represent a nation, revel in killing the innocent, and refuse to wear uniforms—do not qualify for protections under Geneva."[28] But it did not use the resulting opening to rally the international community around a new, internationally accepted terrorism standard—or to compel the various terrorist groups arrayed against it to modify their behavior in response. Today, the Obama White House has the opportunity to do so. At the same time, it will need to take the lead in reforming the global institutions that will be tasked with implementing this new definition.

WATCHING THE WATCHMEN

In 1986, DC Comics, the company made famous by its iconic Superman character, launched a twelve-issue limited series entitled *Watchmen*. Set against a bleak, pre-apocalyptic landscape in which the United States and the Soviet Union were inching ever closer to nuclear annihilation, the story revolves around a group of deeply flawed superheroes caught between helping mankind and serving as its undoing. On the surface, *Watchmen* may have been pulp fare, but its message was very adult: without constraints, the corruption of power can make enemies out of even the best-intentioned. Or, in scribe Alan Moore's modern interpretation of the classical Latin phrase, "Who watches the watchmen?"

That question could be asked of today's United Nations. In 1919, attempting to drum up national support for the League of Nations, President Woodrow Wilson depicted the UN's precursor as a vehicle for international peace, intended to cause "a readjustment of those great injustices which underlay the whole structure of European and Asiatic societies."[29] Twenty-six years later, that same optimism was present at the creation of the United Nations, which was intended as a means "to save succeeding generations from the scourge of war" and as a reaffirmation of "faith in fundamental human rights, in the dignity and worth of the human person, [and] in the equal rights of men and women and of nations large and small."[30]

Today, United Nations officials still pay lip service to these goals. In practice, however, their organization has transformed into a sprawling, unaccountable bureaucracy that in many instances exacerbates the very international problems that it purports to address. And nothing so eloquently epitomizes the rot that has taken hold at Turtle Bay than the single largest corruption scandal in modern history: the one surrounding the UN's Oil-for-Food program.

From the start, Oil-for-Food had been controversial. Between 1996 and 2003, the UN program oversaw some $69 billion in Iraqi oil sales, more than $39 billion in relief purchases, and several billion more for relief works—all the while taking 2.2 percent, more than $1 billion in all, as commission. The lucrative nature of the program—and its gradual expansion to include items beyond what could be strictly termed "humanitarian" in nature—led many observers to conclude that assistance to Iraq had become a get-rich-quick scheme for officials at Turtle Bay.[31]

Information unearthed by the new Iraqi government following the overthrow of Saddam Hussein in 2003 only served to confirm these suspicions. In the months after liberation, the Iraqi Governing Council began to release documents and information about how the former regime had systematically used the Oil-for-Food program to subvert international sanctions, strengthen its hold on power, and amass major wealth at the expense of its countrymen. The revelations touched off an international scandal, which was only exacerbated by the Iraqi Oil Ministry's January 2004 disclosure of some 270 names of those who had benefited from Oil-for-Food corruption. The culprits included numerous oil firms, politicians, and political parties in Russia, China, France, and a host of Middle Eastern nations.[32]

In 2004, bowing to the resulting public pressure, UN Secretary General Kofi Annan appointed an independent commission, headed by former U.S. Federal Reserve Chief Paul Volker, to probe the alleged improprieties within Oil-for-Food. The results were devastating; in its final report, issued the following year, the Volcker Commission disclosed that more than 2,200 firms had made illicit payments to the Saddam Hussein regime between 1997 and 2003, providing the Iraqi dictator with a windfall of close to $2 billion in the process.[33] The revelations led the *Wall Street Journal* to conclude that "Oil for Food is not about some isolated incidents of perceived or actual wrongdoing. . . . Oil for

Food is a story about what the U.N. *is*. And our conclusion . . . is that the U.N. *is* Oil for Food."[34]

Oil-for-Food may have been the most conspicuous scandal to rock the international community's trust in the United Nations in recent years, but it is hardly the only one. The giant Ponzi scheme that allowed UN officials, corrupt foreign politicians, and the Iraqi regime to get rich in spite of international sanctions is just the most visible in a series of instances of official malfeasance on the part of the UN. From graft to the coddling of rogue regimes to the mismanagement of deadly weapons of mass destruction, there is no shortage of evidence that today's United Nations has in many ways become the inverse of Woodrow Wilson's ideal of global justice.

Not surprisingly, more than a few officials have lost their faith in the UN. Perhaps the most prominent example of this dissatisfaction took place during the 2008 presidential campaign, when Republican hopeful John McCain famously called for the creation of a "league of democracies" as a competitor to the United Nations in handling an array of international problems.[35] On the surface, McCain's proposal had much to commend it. A new "league of democracies," unhindered by the political gridlock and bureaucratic infighting of the UN, might be able to more effectively rally a coalition to contain Iran's nuclear program, better promote democratic principles worldwide, and implement more robust international counterterrorism measures. Moreover, it could do so without fear of the Cold War status quo politics that dominate the UN Security Council, where Russia and China have mercilessly wielded their veto power to delay and derail such efforts in the past.

But the costs of such a venture, both political and economic, are likely to be steep. As informed observers have noted, such a construct could worsen Washington's already strained relations with Moscow, and upend its ties with Beijing. It also is likely to be a hard sell with the very countries the United States would need to corral into its new league: the democracies in Europe and Asia, who are in fact deeply ambivalent about marginalizing or replacing the United Nations outright.[36]

They have good reason to be. America may already be a heavyweight in international politics, wielding a permanent seat on the Security Council and the veto power to go along with it. But others are not, and many aspire to this status. Japan, for example, has made the idea of an expanded Security Council, in which it has a permanent seat, a major facet of its foreign policy over the past decade.[37] As a result, Tokyo, for all of its warm relations with Washington, is unlikely to forfeit the equities it has amassed at the UN over the past half-century in favor of a new and unproven organization.

Besides, the UN has the power to serve as a powerful force multiplier for U.S. counterterrorism efforts. Conventional wisdom has it that the United Nations is at best a bystander in the War on Terror. At worst, it is an impediment—a diplomatic obstacle in America's struggle to identify and confront the forces of radical Islam. The reality, however, is a good deal more encouraging.

Via two dedicated antiterrorist bodies—the al-Qaeda and Taliban Sanctions Committee (established pursuant to resolution 1267 in October 1999) and the Counter-Terrorism Committee (created by resolution 1373, less than a month after the September 11 attacks)—the UN has compiled a comprehensive blacklist that has helped impede the ability of terrorist organizations and their affiliates to travel and trade freely. As of this writing, it has created sixteen separate international agreements dealing with counterterrorism, including the landmark 1971 convention which rendered obsolete the practice of airline hijacking. Its range of specialized agencies, meanwhile, provides key services, from port security to counternarcotics training, for countries where for either political or practical reasons the United States cannot.[38] This elaborate counterterrorism structure can be put to the service of America's struggle, if the United States can prompt greater accountability on the part of the UN.

Fortunately, Washington has a great deal of leverage to do so. America currently shoulders a disproportionate amount of the fiscal burden associated with keeping the United Nations in business. In 2006, the U.S. provided more than $5.3 billion to the UN system, including nearly half of the budget of the World Food Programme and roughly a quarter of the UN's entire peacekeeping budget.[39] In the past, some policymakers have suggested that a reduction—or an outright withholding—of this financial commitment could provide a much-needed behavioral corrective.[40] But, as a rule, the U.S. government has failed to consistently adhere to such demands for accountability, preferring consensus in international governance to the prospect of painful and acrimonious debates over the conduct of the world's most powerful forum.

This was true even during the tenure of George W. Bush, who was roundly and routinely lambasted for his perceived "unilateralism." In 2005, Bush broke openly with his own party to oppose a bill that would have slashed America's contribution to the UN system in half if the international body failed to enact a series of budgetary and managerial reforms. The administration's rationale, then–Under Secretary of State for Political Affairs Nicholas Burns told the Senate Foreign Relations Committee at the time, was that such a scaling back of America's commitment would make the UN "less successful."[41]

Perhaps it would. But performance of the sort seen from the UN over the past decade is in sore need of greater oversight—and greater accountability. America, with its unsurpassed influence in the United Nations system, is in a unique position to press for greater transparency, lustration, and reform. It can also harness the UN's latent counterterrorism potential to bolster its efforts to constrict the operating environment for its terrorist adversaries.

Such steps are not just vital to American interests. They are essential to the continued relevance of the United Nations as well. As former House Speaker Newt Gingrich, the co-chair of the congressionally mandated Task Force on American Interests and UN Reform, told the Senate Foreign Relations Committee in July 2005, a fundamental transformation of the way the UN does business is necessary if it is "to become an effective instrument in protecting the safety of the American people and the dignity of peoples worldwide." Otherwise, "the U.N. will remain an uncertain instrument, both for the governments that comprise it and for those that look to it for salvation."[42]

NOTES

1. R. James Woolsey, remarks at the American Foreign Policy Council conference on "Understanding the Iranian Threat," Washington, DC, November 15, 2006.

2. Sayyid Qutb, *In the Shade Of The Koran*, vol. 5 (Markfield, Leicester: The Islamic Foundation, 2002), 312.

3. "Ahmadinejad: Wipe Israel off Map," *Al-Jazeera* (Doha), October 26, 2005, http://english.aljazeera.net/NR/exeres/15E6BF77-6F91-46EE-A4B5-A3CE0E9957EA.htm.

4. William Wunderle and Gabriel Lajeunesse, "Winning the Next War," *The Journal of International Security Affairs* 15 (2008): 111.

5. *Constitution of the United States of America*, Article II, Section 2, Clause 2, September 17, 1787.

6. *Charter of the United Nations*, Article 2, June 26, 1945.

7. Thomas Aquinas, *The Summa Theologica* (New York: Benziger Brothers., 1947), Part II, Question 40.

8. Ken Webb, "The Classical Just War Doctrine: *Jus in Bello*," *Oriens* 11, no. 2 (2006), http://www.oriensjournal.com/webb.html.

9. Allah Bukhsh K. Brohi, "Preface," in S. K. Malik, *The Quranic Concept of War* (New Delhi: Adam, 1992).

10. See, for example, Fawaz A. Gerges, *The Far Enemy: How Jihad Went Global* (Cambridge: Cambridge University Press, 2005), 9–10.

11. Majid Khadduri, *War and Peace in the Law of Islam* (Baltimore: The Johns Hopkins Press, 1955), 16.

12. Brohi, "Preface."

13. Muhammad Khalil al-Hakaymah, "Toward a New Strategy in Resisting the Occupier," in Jim Lacey, ed., *The Canons of Jihad: Terrorists' Strategy for Defeating America* (Annapolis, MD: Naval Institute Press, 2008), 155.

14. As cited in Middle East Media Research Institute *Special Dispatch* 917, June 7, 2005, http://mcmri.org/bin/articles.cgi?P...a‑sd&ID‑SP91705.

15. Bin Laden's communiqué was cited in the indictment of Zacarias Moussaoui, the suspected twentieth September 11 hijacker, that was handed down by the U.S. District Court for the Eastern District of Virginia in December 2001. The indictment can be accessed online at http://www.usdoj.gov/ag/moussaoui indictment.htm.

16. *Constitution of the Islamic Republic of Iran*, Preamble, October 24, 1979.

17. As cited in Center for Special Studies, Intelligence and Terrorism Information Center, "Hezbollah," July 2003, http://www.intelligence.org.il/eng/bu/hizbullah/pb/app13.htm.

18. Benjamin Wittes, *Law and the Long War: The Future of Justice in the Age of Terrorism* (New York: Penguin, 2008), 19–43.

19. President George W. Bush, "Military Order—Detention, Treatment and Trial of Certain Non-Citizens in the War against Terrorism," November 13, 2001, as published in the *Federal Register* 66, no. 222 (2001): 57831.

20. *Hamdan v. Rumsfeld*, 415 F. 3d 33 (2006). The Court's opinion can be found at http://www.cbsnews.com/htdocs/pdf/Hamdan_vs_Rumsfeld.pdf.

21. Andrew C. McCarthy, "The Myth of Bush's Torture Regime," *National Review* 60, no. 24 (2008), http://www.defenddemocracy.org/index .php?option=com_content&task=view&id=11784123&Itemid=0; See also Andrew C. McCarthy, "Geneva and Savagery," *National Review Online*, June 20, 2006, http://www.defenddemocracy.org/index.php?option=com_content&task =view&id=11777470&Itemid=0.

22. Charles Babington and Michael Abramowitz, "U.S. Shifts Policy on Geneva Conventions," *Washington Post*, July 12, 2006, A01.

23. Mark Mazetti and William Glaberson, "Obama Issues Directive to Shut Down Guantanamo," *New York Times*, January 21, 2009, http://www.nytimes.com/2009/01/22/us/politics/22gitmo.html?_r=3&hp.

24. "Blair: Army Interrogation Manual to Apply to CIA," Associated Press, January 22, 2009, http://www.google.com/hostednews/ap/article/ALeqM5jukrb8-2-9wVR1JcQ6G0sZBQr6OwD95SACFG0.

25. McCarthy, "The Myth of Bush's Torture Regime."

26. *Charter of the United Nations*, Article 1, June 26, 1945.

27. For a sampling of these targets, see Australia/Israel & Jewish Affairs Council, "Hezbollah Attacks Since May 2000," July 24, 2006, http://www.aijac.org.au/resources/hezb_00-06.html.

28. Babington and Abramowitz, "U.S. Shifts Policy on Geneva Conventions."

29. Woodrow Wilson, speech before the City Auditorium in Pueblo, Colorado, September 25, 1919, as reprinted in Arthur S. Link, ed., *The Papers of Woodrow Wilson* vol. 63 (Princeton: Princeton University Press, 1990), 500–13.

30. *Charter of the United Nations*, Preamble, June 26, 1945.

31. See, for example, Claudia Rosett, "Oil for Food, Money for Kofi," *Weekly Standard* 8, no. 24 (2003): 16–17.

32. *Al-Mada* (Baghdad), January 25, 2004 (author's collection).

33. "2,200 Firms Paid Saddam Bribes: Report," *The Age* (Melbourne), October 27, 2005, http://www.theage.com.au/news/World/2200-firms-paid-Saddam-bribes-report/2005/10/27/1130382514669.html.

34. Review and Outlook, "Oil for Food as Usual," *Wall Street Journal*, September 9, 2005, http://www.opinionjournal.com/editorial/feature.html?id=110007229.

35. Liz Sidoti, "McCain Favors A 'League of Democracies,'" Associated Press, April 30, 2007, http://www.washingtonpost.com/wp-dyn/content/article/2007/04/30/AR2007043001402.html.

36. Gideon Rachman, "Why McCain's Big Idea is a Bad Idea," *Financial Times* (London), May 6, 2008, 11.

37. See, for example, Hiroko Tabuchi, "Japan's Security Council Seat Less Likely," Associated Press, August 24, 2005, http://seattletimes.nwsource.com/html/nationworld/2002450215_japan24.html.

38. The International Maritime Organization, for example, currently has extensive interaction with the government of Bashar al-Asad in Syria over maritime security in the port city of Latakia. See United Nations Development Programme, "Syria: Modernization of Syria Maritime-Lattakia Port," n.d., http://www.undp.org.sy/index.php/our-work/business-for-development-/76-modernization-of-syrian-maritime-lattakia-port-syr05019.

39. U.S. Department of State, Office of the Spokesman, "Fact Sheet: The United States and International Development: Partnering for Growth," December

31, 2007, http://usunrome.usmission.gov/viewer/article.asp?idSite=1&article=/file2008_01/alia/a8010202.htm.

40. For example, until his death in 2003, Sen. Jesse Helms (R-NC) was among the fiercest American critics of the United Nations, using his considerable power to block payment of dues as a method of compelling institutional reform.

41. As cited in Deborah Tate, "Bush Officials Repeat Opposition to Effort to Withhold UN Dues," *Voice of America*, July 21, 2005, http://www.voanews.com/english/archive/2005-07/2005-07-21-voa71.cfm.

42. The Honorable Newt Gingrich, testimony before the Senate Committee on Foreign Relations, July 21, 2005, http://foreign.senate.gov/testimony/2005/GingrichTestimony050721.pdf.

6

STRATEGIC
DEMOCRATIZATION

In September 2002, less than a year after taking office, the Bush administration laid out a breathtakingly ambitious vision of American foreign policy. "The United States possesses unprecedented—and unequaled—strength and influence in the world," the newly released *National Security Strategy of the United States of America* proudly proclaimed. "Sustained by faith in the principles of liberty, and the value of a free society, this position comes with unparalleled responsibilities, obligations, and opportunity. The great strength of this nation must be used to promote a balance of power that favors freedom."[1] Over the next several years, this focus spawned an ambitious "freedom agenda," encompassing the creation of multiple new institutions (among them the Middle East Partnership Initiative, the Millennium Challenge Corporation, and the Middle East Free Trade Initiative) and a financial commitment of over a billion dollars annually.

Yet, these days, despite the efforts of the Bush administration, democracy does not appear to be on the march. True, the Bush administration's first term saw a number of notable democratic transformations: Georgia's "Rose" Revolution in 2003, Ukraine's "Orange" Revolution in 2004, and the "Tulip" and "Cedar" Revolutions that took place in Kyrgyzstan and Lebanon, respectively, in 2005. But, as the human rights watchdog Freedom Watch noted in its most recent survey on the subject, the years since have seen a decline in "global freedom."[2]

Evidence of this backward momentum abounds. In places such as Afghanistan, the demise of the old, radical regime has been replaced by widespread political instability that threatens to undermine the fledgling postauthoritarian order. In a host of others—from Russia to Zimbabwe—already repressive governments are putting into place new restrictions on political thought, freedom of expression, and the ability of their citizens to organize.[3] Meanwhile, Islamist forces, many of them deeply antagonistic to democratic principles, have succeeded in making significant political inroads throughout the Muslim world.

TRIAL AND ERROR

Just where and how did things go wrong? Some answers can be found in the common misconceptions, which have permeated official Washington in recent years, about the mechanisms by which to foster—and, more importantly, to sustain—democracy abroad.[4]

The first has to do with confusion about the proper role of democracy in American policy. As a *tactic*, democracy promotion can be an effective tool. After all, the character of individual regimes matters a great deal. Governments that are unaccountable to their own people are far more susceptible to corruption and radicalism, and are more likely to engage in criminal behavior.[5] It is not by accident that the world's leading state sponsors of terrorism are today all governed by deeply authoritarian, highly unrepresentative regimes. Democracies, by contrast, make better counterterrorism partners. Because an enfranchised populace becomes a stakeholder in a stable civil society, it is by its nature more sensitive to the threats posed by political radicals. And, since democracy demands a greater degree of transparency and accountability from its government, citizens are far less likely to allow their leaders to provide aid and comfort to fringe groups.

The adoption of democracy as *strategy*, however, is far more problematic. It makes the promotion of democratic processes abroad an overriding priority for U.S. foreign policy—a choice that, by necessity, wreaks havoc upon existing alliance structures and distorts the economics of American engagement abroad. For, while "tactical democracy," if used selectively and carefully, can be a potent weapon against extremism, a policy that promotes democracy above all other priorities is at best counterproductive. At worst, it is downright dangerous.

Early on, the Bush administration showed encouraging signs of understanding this distinction. In the days after September 11, it launched its campaign in Afghanistan not because the regime there was undemocratic, a state of affairs that had persisted for decades, but because of the latter's role in harboring and facilitating the activities of the al-Qaeda terrorist network. Upon the Taliban's ouster, President Bush threw his weight behind interim leader Hamid Karzai, in large part because he was committed to preventing his country from becoming a safe haven for terrorism—a goal Karzai sought to accomplish through the creation of a pluralistic governing system. In other words, the orienting principle of U.S. policy vis-à-vis Afghanistan was, and remains, counterterrorism, although the promotion of democratic principles represents an important part of that policy.

Very quickly thereafter, however, the Bush administration began to show signs of mission creep. The elevation of democracy to the status of grand strategy first became visible in the context of Iraq in February 2003, when the President himself told the American Enterprise Institute in Washington that "[s]uccess in Iraq could also begin a new stage for Middle Eastern peace, and set in motion progress towards a truly democratic Palestinian state."[6] In the years that followed, the Bush White House time and again emphasized the centrality of democracy (rather than stability) in Iraq to its vision of a prosperous region.[7]

This conflation of goals belied a deep confusion about the dynamics of the Middle East, where a myriad of other issues, from the succession question in Egypt to the long-term stability of the House of Saud, also require Washington's attention. It also connotes enormous opportunity costs. Until 2007, when the Bush administration defied conventional wisdom (and the suggestions of nearly all of its professional military advisors) and instituted a "surge" of troops in Iraq, it was far from clear that that country could in fact emerge as a viable, functioning, and pluralistic state. Today, such a lasting outcome is still far from assured. Much will depend on the shape and pace of America's withdrawal from Iraq, and a mature and lasting assumption of power by the Iraqi government. In conceptual terms, however, the damage has already been done. At least in the view of some skeptics, "[t]he Bush administration's close identification of democracy building with the war in Iraq has discredited the concept both at home and abroad."[8]

The second problem facing American officials has been a failure to understand that democracy is a process as well as a destination. All too often, U.S. policymakers have lauded signs of movement toward pluralism in foreign lands, only to fail in providing the political and economic support needed to sustain such trends over time.

Ukraine serves as a perfect example of this attention deficit disorder. In November 2004, the elevation of former foreign minister Viktor Yanukovych to the country's presidency in controversial elections blatantly manipulated by Moscow brought hundreds of thousands to the streets in an outpouring of protest that became known as the "Orange Revolution." The protesters succeeded beyond their wildest dreams; over the course of two months, the original results of the vote were annulled and a new election held. In it, popular, Western-leaning Viktor Yushchenko handily defeated Yanukovych in what was widely seen as a referendum for a new national direction—one free of Russian influence.

In the West, the outcome was hailed as a major success for democratic forces. During the heady days of the "Orange Revolution," a number of American nongovernmental organizations (including the National Democratic Institute and the International Republican Institute) had played a major—albeit quiet—role in organizing and sustaining the civic campaign against Yanukovych,[9] with tacit approval from the U.S. government. Yet, in the wake of Yushchenko's electoral victory, Washington's attention seemed to waver. Financially, the U.S. government remained invested; when tallied in September 2008, U.S. aid to Ukraine since 2005 was calculated at some $350 million.[10] Politically, however, the appearance of Washington's disengagement from post-revolution Ukrainian politics left reformers with the unmistakable impression that they had been forgotten.

That feeling proved fatal. Left to their own devices, Ukraine's various political blocs dissolved into bitter factional infighting. That disorder, in turn, allowed revanchist forces within the Ukrainian body politic, buoyed by a refocused Russia, to grow increasingly powerful. The culmination came in March 2006, when parliamentary elections abruptly swept Yushchenko's administration from office in favor of a coalition government headed by none other than his bitter political rival, Viktor Yanukovych. In less than a year-and-a-half, the "Orange Revolution" suffered a near-total reversal of fortune—the political instability from which still lingers in Kyiv today.

The experience of Ukraine serves as a cautionary tale. Today, the United States has unrivaled capability to support liberal democratic forces around the world. Such support, however, cannot be short-term. Neither should it be pegged to the attainment of any one particular political objective or goal. Rather, it needs to be sustained in nature, and calibrated to empower not only the initial successes of reformers, but the preservation of these victories over time as well.

The third challenge confronting American policymakers is the arduous task of political capacity-building. In order for democracy to thrive in the historically inhospitable soil of the Middle East, the people on the Arab and Muslim streets must perceive that they have real choices about exactly who governs them and what shape that government will take.

In principle, the United States has understood the need to inject new voices in the Middle Eastern political debate. In its public discourse, the Bush administration repeatedly emphasized the importance of reformers and political progressives to the creation of a new, more pluralistic order in the region.[11] As a practical matter, however, recent years have seen precious little investment of this sort on the part of the United States.

Events in the Palestinian Authority are emblematic of this failure. The United States and its allies were taken by surprise when Hamas, the radical Palestinian offshoot of Egypt's Muslim Brotherhood, abruptly swept to power in the Palestinian Authority in early 2006, but they should not have been. When Palestinians went to the polls in the West Bank and Gaza Strip in January 2006, they had been presented with just two choices, President Mahmoud Abbas' sclerotic Fatah party or its Islamist opposition. The decision was not a difficult one to make.

After all, Fatah had maintained a virtual monopoly on power in the West Bank and Gaza Strip ever since Yasser Arafat's return to the Palestinian Territories in 1994. The following twelve years saw an institutionalization and expansion of the crony politics, corruption, and authoritarianism that characterized PLO practices—all carried out at the expense of ordinary Palestinians. Hamas, meanwhile, had deftly stepped into the vacuum left by Arafat's rogue regime, expanding its role in Palestinian education, medicine, and social services. In the process, it positioned itself as a viable political alternative to the PLO. Thus, when it came time for Palestinians to choose, they avoided the corrupt, secular government that had robbed them in favor of an Islamist one that they hoped would not.

None of this registered on Washington's radar. In the run-up to the Palestinian vote, U.S. officials were quick to express their support for the beleaguered government of Mahmoud Abbas, and just as quick to warn of dire international consequences, from political ostracism to a cut-off of international aid, should Hamas be elected. They did not, however, devote their energies to forcing Fatah to implement the kind of grassroots anti-corruption measures that might have shored up its flagging domestic popularity. Neither did the United States expend the time or effort necessary to foster serious political competition that could have served to supplant—or at least dilute—the appeal of Hamas. And, by failing to do so, Washington inadvertently helped to midwife the birth of a radical Islamist government committed to the destruction of its neighbor in part of the Palestinian Territories.

Fourth, when Washington does choose to promote democratic principles abroad, it must be discriminating about where and how it does so. In order to be prudent and sustainable, democracy assistance needs to be judiciously weighed against other pressing foreign policy priorities involving the nation or nations in question.

Some scholars faulted the Bush administration for exactly this focus. "[T]he fight against al Qaeda," the Carnegie Endowment's Thomas Carothers pointed out back in 2003, "tempts Washington to put aside its democratic scruples and seek closer ties with autocracies throughout the Middle East and Asia."[12] This is certainly true, to an extent. While it lasted, Washington's post–September 11 partnership with Pakistani strongman Pervez Musharraf, for example, had little to do with a fondness for the wily General himself and everything to do with U.S. fears of what could happen should the country's Islamist forces take over. U.S. pressure on Saudi Arabia's rulers to reform has similarly been nominal, due in no small measure to Riyadh's importance in the overall American energy calculus.

Just as often, however, the Bush administration leaned in exactly the opposite direction. It exerted pressure on foreign governments to reform, often at the expense of other strategic initiatives or priorities. Nowhere was this more pronounced than with regard to Russia. From early cooperation in the War on Terror, relations between Moscow and Washington have deteriorated into mutual recriminations and discord over Russia's domestic practices. As Vice President Dick Cheney remarked at the May 2006 Vilnius Conference, in Russia today "opponents of reform are seeking to reverse the gains of the last decade. In many areas of civil society—from religion and the news media, to advocacy groups and political parties—the government has unfairly and improperly restricted the rights of her people." Russia, Cheney concluded, "has a choice to make. And there is no question that a return to democratic reform in Russia will generate further success for its people and greater respect among fellow nations."[13]

Cheney's concerns were certainly well-placed. Nor were they unique. Over the past three years, a growing chorus of statesmen and politicians from both sides of the political aisle has raised concerns about the increasingly authoritarian, unrepresentative, and repressive nature of the Russian government under Vladimir Putin and his handpicked protégé, Dmitry Medvedev. But for the foreseeable future, the United States has neither the capacity nor the inclination to aggressively promote democratic processes within the Russian Federation. It does, however, desperately need Moscow's aid and backing to resolve a number of pressing international issues, chief among them the twin nuclear crises of North Korea and Iran. And such cooperation is far less likely to be forthcoming from a government that has been internationally vilified by the United States for its questionable internal conduct.

When it comes to democracy promotion, in other words, Washington must pick and choose its battles. If it does not, it runs the risk of alienating potential partners on any number of foreign policy fronts—making its strategic objectives all the more difficult to attain.

In the years ahead, American democracy promotion efforts will need to correct these deficiencies. They will also need to focus on two new priorities, both of which are critical to the success of efforts to promote pluralism and tolerance throughout the world.

MINDING THE (EDUCATION) GAP

Why do they hate us? In the days after September 11, that was the question preoccupying many Americans struggling to comprehend the atrocities that had been perpetrated by al-Qaeda and applauded throughout the Muslim world. Early on, many seized upon the idea that poverty and a lack of economic opportunity lay behind the animus visible in much of the Middle East and beyond.

This, however, turned out to be incorrect. As Middle East scholar Daniel Pipes noted back in 2003, "the empirical record evinces little correlation between economics and militant Islam."[14] Indeed, as many have since noted, the September 11 hijackers were, almost to a man, the products of middle- and upper-class upbringings in their native countries; children of privilege, rather than privation. This example, and myriad others, suggests that:

> Aggregate measures of wealth and economic trends fall flat as predictors of where militant Islam will be strong and where not. On the level of individuals, too, conventional wisdom points to militant Islam attracting the poor, the alienated and the marginal—but research finds precisely the opposite to be true. To the extent that economic factors explain who becomes Islamist, they point to the fairly well off, not the poor.[15]

If the connection between poverty and militancy is tenuous, however, the one between radicalism and education is more causal. Pakistan provides what is perhaps the clearest case in point. Over the past three decades, Pakistan's educational sector has steadily atrophied, a casualty of neglect and partisan politics.[16] This state of affairs has prompted the rise of a parallel religious education system built around a specialized Islamic curriculum known as the *Dars-e Nizami*. Ostensibly, other subjects—including mathematics, history, and medicine—are also offered. But specialists are quick to point out that this falls far short of a "well-rounded education," since all the texts used for instruction, even those for supposedly "rational sciences," are fundamentalist in nature, and many have stopped being taught altogether in Pakistan's ten thousand *madaris* (the plural of *madrassa*).[17]

Of these, Darul Uloom Haqqania in the Northwest Frontier Province is among the most prominent. In the past, Darul Uloom is known to have served as training ground for Taliban leaders, as well as a recruiting center for Pakistani militants fighting in Kashmir.[18] Today, Darul Uloom still casts a long ideological shadow; more than 2,800 Pakistani, Afghan, Tajik, Kazakh, Uzbek, and Chechen students are currently estimated to be enrolled there.[19] Another are the Ahle-hadith *madaris*, located outside of Lahore, which have provided fighters to the Kashmiri terrorist group Lashkar-e Taiba.[20]

By objective standards, the size of the problem is small. Officials in Islamabad estimate that some 1.7 million students—just one percent of the country's population—are enrolled in the *madrassa* system.[21] Yet if even a fraction of that number becomes radicalized enough to join the jihad against the West, it would be a boon to terrorist groups such as al-Qaeda and a major challenge to the United States and its allies. And by all indications, that is precisely what is happening in places such as Afghanistan and Kashmir, where anecdotal evidence suggests that local radicals are being reinforced by new recruits from Pakistan's Islamic schools.

Pakistan may be the most prominent example of this radicalization, but it is hardly the only one. Indeed, the same conditions that empowered the rise of a parallel, largely unaccountable educational system there can be seen today throughout the Arab and Islamic worlds.

It was not always this way. Between the eighth and tenth centuries, Islamic thinkers pioneered significant new knowledge in mathematics and astronomy. The same period saw the translation and dissemination of classic books of literature and Greek philosophy throughout the Muslim world, and new inventions that aided technological and scientific discovery.[22] Subsequent years, however, saw a systematic closing of the Muslim mind, as the "gates" of *ijtihad*—open, scholarly interpretation of Quranic texts—were "closed" and clerical authority replaced intellectual inquiry.[23]

The cumulative effects of this change have been profound. Today, specialists say, the Muslim world suffers from a "crisis of education"—one that has systematically stripped that part of the world from effectively competing in the "geography of ideas."[24] Exactly how deep this crisis runs is painfully clear. In its 2008 report on educational reform in the Middle East and North Africa, the World Bank notes that the countries of the region as a whole score far below countries like Chile and Estonia in every area of "knowledge"—from the skills and education level of their populations to the presence of an infrastructure that reinforces and rewards learning.[25] Adult illiteracy in Arab states, meanwhile, stands at some 50 percent, nearly double that of the rest of the Third World.[26] The Islamic world, in other words, is an intellectual outlier, an area of the planet that has failed to keep pace with others in the arena of thoughts, ideas, and innovation.

This state of affairs represents a major challenge for the West. According to the World Bank, "the population of 15-to-24-year-olds accounts for 21.5 percent (approximately 70 million) of the regional population, while another 45 percent is less than 15 years of age."[27] In practical terms, this means that more than half of the entire Middle East and North Africa is of school age, and will continue to be for at least another generation. Yet America so far has paid far too little attention to this "youth bulge" or the means by which it could shape its upbringing and outlook. When tallied in mid-2008, the U.S. government's total investment in basic education worldwide stood at approximately

$1.75 billion. Of that sum, just over a third ($650 million) was spent in the Islamic world.[28] Yet this outreach, when it has taken place, has been both uneven and politicized. Of the world's forty-nine majority Muslim countries and territories, nearly 40 percent do not receive American basic educational assistance.[29] Rather, U.S. education assistance is allocated based, above all, on the recipient country's ability to provide "return on the dollar," with little attention given its importance to the overall battle of ideas taking place in the Islamic world. Perhaps the most emblematic—and egregious—example of this trend is the fact that, since 2005, the U.S. government, as a matter of official government policy, has funded no basic education programs in what is arguably the central battlefield of our fight against al-Qaeda: Iraq (although U.S. military commanders there retain considerable authority to undertake such projects on their own).[30]

This amounts to a fatal error. Without precisely these sorts of investments, the overwhelmingly young population of the Muslim world will be forced to rely on local—and often radical—interpretations of the world, and their place in it. And, as we have discovered all too well in recent years, no shortage of those exist.

Just days after taking office in January 2001, President Bush unveiled an ambitious agenda for bipartisan education reform, at the core of which lay the conviction that the level of basic education within the United States needed to be improved and standardized.[31] In the years since, this program—commonly known as "No Child Left Behind"—has seen no small measure of controversy. But its basic premise, that the road to national prosperity leads through the education of, and engagement with, the country's youth, still rings true.

Today, America needs to make a similar commitment to fostering education in the Muslim world. From alternative textbooks that promote moderate Islamic ideas to new "knowledge" infrastructure designed to increase intellectual curiosity and market competitiveness, the United States has the economic ability to make major upgrades to regional education. What it has lacked so far is the political will to do so, and an accurate understanding of why such investments are in fact critical to American national security.

The answer is obvious. The educational vacuum that now prevails throughout the Muslim world has permitted a plethora of radical ideologies and intolerant ideas to take root, and wooed untold numbers of converts to the cause of America's adversaries. Without greater investments in regional education, the United States will continue to remain a marginal force on this field of battle, much to the detriment of its own security and to the prosperity of Muslim nations.

OUTMANEUVERING ISLAMISTS AT THE BALLOT BOX

Perhaps the most fundamental challenge facing the United States in its struggle against radical Islam, however, lies at the polls. Over the past several years, Islamists of various stripes have begun to discover that they can advance their political and ideological agendas far more effectively through the ballot box than they can on the battlefield. As a result, there is now a "near-consensus among mainstream Islamist leaders in key Arab countries and Turkey on the value of democratic participation—that is, contestation for power via competitive elections," a July 2005 study by the congressionally funded United States Institute of Peace found.[32]

And they are succeeding. Egypt's powerful Muslim Brotherhood movement shocked observers in December 2005 when—despite being formally banned from national politics—it managed to capture nearly a fifth of the seats in the country's parliament through elections. Even more successful has been Hezbollah, the powerful Shi'ite militia established in Lebanon with Iran's guidance in the early 1980s. Once strictly an opposition movement, Hezbollah now operates as a full-fledged political party in Beirut—and as a virtual government in Lebanon's south, where the ambit of the central government does not fully extend.

Arguably the biggest success story, however, has taken place in Turkey, where a wily Islamist faction, the Justice and Development Party (AKP), has been ensconced since unexpectedly coming to power in late 2002. In July 2007, the AKP scored a resounding electoral victory over its secularist opponents, garnering nearly 47 percent of the popular vote and securing 341 seats in the country's 550-seat parliament. Coming as it did on the heels of a heated political tug-of-war with its main political rival, the Turkish military, the AKP's gains were seen both as a sign of its popularity and of its political savvy.

The political victories of these groups have a great deal to do with the tactics they employ. Islamists, says Egyptian political scientist Mona Makram-Ebcid, "have managed to incorporate key elements of the liberal platform in their agenda: demands for accountability, constitutional reform, an end to political repression, and clean and uncorrupt government."[33] These talking points have allowed them to outmaneuver their respective governments, portraying them as corrupt, venal, and unrepresentative—often with good reason. And, because more often than not the United States is engaged with those regimes in some way, Islamist political factions have quickly learned to add another element to their repertoire: anti-Americanism.

The response from the West has been feeble. Scholars and officials alike have generally taken a benign view of the evolution of Islamist tactics, equating them with signs of moderation.[34] The preponderance of the evidence, however, suggests that political participation does not automatically translate into a softening of ideological or political principles. Thus, when it finally went public with its long-awaited draft political platform in October 2007, the Muslim Brotherhood dismayed many reformists by advocating an exclusionary clerical state similar to the Iranian theocracy.[35] Similarly, Hezbollah remains committed to the destruction of Israel and the United States, despite its prominent role in Lebanese politics.[36] Turkey's AKP, meanwhile, has waged a concerted assault on the secular institutions of Mustafa Kemal Attaturk's republic since taking power in 2002, using the criteria required by the European Union for Turkey's entry to progressively erase the dividing lines between mosque and state.[37]

This state of affairs should not be surprising. After all, to the extent that they present competing principles for social development, democracy and Islam are in conflict. The former centers on the importance of individual rights and free will; the latter revolves around the subjugation of those principles to divine edict, or at least to a particular interpretation of it. All of which goes a long way toward explaining why groups such as al-Qaeda are so opposed to—and threatened by—Western liberalism. As the late, unlamented leader of al-Qaeda in Iraq, Abu Musab al-Zarqawi, put it back in 2005, "[w]e have declared a bitter war against the principle of democracy and all those who seek to enact it."[38]

Al-Qaeda's vision is certainly not universally accepted, or even all that popular among the majority of Muslims. Yet even less absolutist Islamic political factions are unequivocal in their interpretations of the proper place of religion in society. Thus, despite its drift toward participation in Egypt's political system, the Muslim Brotherhood is adamant that that system should ultimately be transformed into a "true Islamic government," and makes no secret of the fact that its ultimate objective is "mastering the world with Islam."[39] Even the far more subtle strain of political Islam espoused by Turkey's AKP envisions the transformation of Mustafa Kemal's Ataturk's secular republic into an "Islamic state."[40]

So far, Washington has failed to formulate a serious response to the political inroads made by Islamists in these places, and in others. Rather, America's very proper insistence on the importance of democratic processes has forced it to support those that employ these methods, even when their ultimate end goals are blatantly undemocratic. In the process, the United States has defined democracy down—abiding, and even encouraging, those who talk the democratic talk but walk a profoundly different walk.

If it hopes to outmaneuver Islamists at the ballot box, the United States will need to change tacks. Rather than simply acquiescing to the gains of Islamists who mouth support for democratic processes, Washington should force these factions to prove it by instituting constitutional protections and enshrining political checks and balances that make the subversion of the current system, if not impossible, then far less likely.

At the same time, the United States will need to work to pluralize the political dialogue in the greater Middle East. The old axiom that one should keep friends close and enemies closer is applicable to the politics of the Islamic world, where today authoritarian governments operate with scant political opposition and fewer institutional constraints on their rule. This polarized political field has allowed Islamist movements to thrive, not because of the inherent appeal of their ideas but because they serve as the only viable outlet for expression among those who are opposed to official policy. The key to diminishing their stature, therefore, lies in forcing their adherence to an existing political process where their ideas can stand or fall based upon real public scrutiny.

Most of all, however, the United States needs to communicate to these countries and constituencies, directly and by example, that what makes America unique, and its mode of government so revered, is not simply democratic principles but the open society in which they operate, where individual freedoms are protected, where popular will guides policy, and where everyone agrees to play by the rules of the civic game. If it does not, the U.S. principle of "one man, one vote" could soon take on a very different meaning in the Muslim world: "one man, one vote, one time."

CHAPTER 6

REGIME CHANGE, REVISITED

A final topic that deserves consideration is the question of regime change. The Bush administration's term in office clearly demonstrated that there was no one definitive way in which governments could be changed. Rather, the period between 2001 and 2008 witnessed three separate and distinct paths to democratic transformation.[41]

The first, seen most clearly in Libya's very public about-face on its nuclear weapons program in 2003, was that governments could transform of their own volition, based on the understanding that internal change was the best—perhaps the only—way of staying in business. The second, borne out by the "color revolutions" that swept over the post-Soviet space between 2003 and 2005, was that a regime could be fundamentally altered by the choices of its own people. The third—and, as the Bush White House made abundantly clear on its watch, the least desirable—was that a regime could be changed by another country through force, if it constituted a clear and present danger to the international order.

And yet, perhaps understandably, it is this third incarnation that has overshadowed the others. In the aftermath of the war in Iraq, "regime change" has become synonymous with the use of military force. And the difficult and bloody path to victory in post-Saddam Iraq has made the possibility that the United States could affect such a transformation elsewhere in the foreseeable future exceedingly unlikely.

But should it be? Today, the United States has no shortage of leverage over the behavior of foreign governments, either by empowering democratic forces or via the application of coercive diplomacy. What it lacks, however, is a serious understanding of how to affect such "regime change" strategically.

Iran is a case in point. Since the Iranian regime was discovered to be pursuing a clandestine nuclear program some six years ago, the international community has been preoccupied with Tehran's seemingly inexorable march toward the bomb. Yet so far, nothing the world has done, on the diplomatic front or any other, has made much difference in the Islamic Republic's strategic calculus.

This has led some to conclude that Iran's nuclear program constitutes a *casus belli* that warrants the use of force.[42] But, as more than a few scholars and experts have pointed out, the scope of the Iranian nuclear effort, and the complexity of concerted action against it, are bound to make any such strike a technically difficult and costly affair. It is also one that, all things considered, the United States is exceedingly unlikely to undertake. The reason lies in the U.S. intelligence community's November 2007 National Intelligence Estimate (NIE), which painted a largely benign view of Iran's nuclear progress to date.[43] Although subsequent studies have cast doubt upon the NIE's conclusions,[44] the political damage has been lasting. As columnist Morton Kondracke put it at the time, the NIE's findings "ended any possibility that Bush could win support for an attack on Iran's nuclear facilities."[45] Bush's successor, meanwhile, has given no indication that he is interested in pursuing such a course of action at all.

Yet, just because military action against Iran appears to be off the table as a serious policy option does not mean that the United States lacks the ability to affect lasting change in Tehran. Indeed, there are at least two concrete ways by which it can do so.

The first deals with altering the behavior of the Iranian regime with regard to its nuclear ambitions. In his 2002 State of the Union Address, President Bush famously identified three countries—Iran, Iraq, and North Korea—as members of an "axis of evil, arming to threaten the peace of the world."[46] Later that same year, one of those countries—North Korea—confronted the United States with an unprecedented challenge when it disclosed that it had clandestinely developed a nuclear capability. North Korea's nuclear breakout has successfully stymied American strategy in Asia ever since, and the lesson has not been lost on Iran's ayatollahs. The Iranian regime has been working tirelessly on its nuclear program, animated by the conviction that it needs to go nuclear like North Korea, lest it end up out of business like Iraq. Simply put, Iran's ayatollahs have become convinced that the stability of their regime is directly correlated to the maturity of their nuclear effort.

The key to chilling Tehran's enthusiasm for "the bomb," therefore, hinges upon inverting that equation. Through a stronger mix of economic measures (such as those discussed in chapter 4), as well as financial/logistical support for diverse opposition groups inside and outside the country, the United States can craft a policy that makes Iran's nuclear progress inversely proportional to regime stability. Such steps, if taken resolutely and explicitly linked to Tehran's nuclear intransigence, will go a long way toward convincing the Iranian regime that if it wants to stay in business, it must get out of the nuclear business.

The second, more fundamental approach, involves changing the character of the Iranian regime itself. After all, the danger that emanates today from the Islamic Republic has everything to do with the nature of the regime there; Iran's enduring support for terrorism abroad, and its persistent nuclear ambitions, are merely manifestations of the radical, expansionist ideology that animates the current regime in Tehran. Therefore, the best way to defuse the contemporary threat posed by the Iranian regime, experts have pointed out, is to change its character—and the best way to do that lies in altering the relationship between the government and its captive population.[47]

That the United States has failed to do so is something of an understatement. Early on, the Bush administration's post–September 11 advocacy of a "forward strategy that favors freedom"[48] fanned hopes among many that—in contrast to its predecessors—it would truly engage with pro-democracy forces within Iran. So did President Bush's calls for the Iranian leadership "to respect the will of its people and be accountable to them."[49] In practice, however, the principles of the "Bush Doctrine" did not extend as far as the Islamic Republic. For all of its lip service to Iranian democracy, the Bush White House offered only nominal aid to those seeking freedom and pluralism within the Islamic Republic. Between 2004 and 2008, it authorized a total of $215 million in funding for all diplomatic programs dealing with Iran. But only a small fraction of that sum—some $38.6 million—was dedicated specifically to democracy promotion.[50] And even those paltry funds ultimately were diluted by bureaucratic infighting that served to undermine their effectiveness.[51]

Today, the Obama administration gives few signs that it plans to support democratic change in Iran more seriously. During the 2008 presidential campaign, then-candidate Barack Obama famously called for a "surge of diplomacy" to mirror the military surge taking place next door in Iraq.[52] Since taking office, the new president has given every indication that he plans to do just that, selecting a seasoned negotiator, Dennis Ross, as his special envoy on the Iranian issue, and moving forward with plans for formal "engagement" with Tehran. Not surprisingly, given this diplomatic focus, little attention has so far been paid to how the United States can effectively empower more democratic alternatives to the current regime in Tehran, even though internal conditions there have never painted a more hopeful picture of Iran's potential for change.

THE ENDURING LOGIC OF DEMOCRACY PROMOTION

Today, it is hard to deny that the idea of democracy promotion has seen better days. Surveying the missteps of the previous administration, some skeptics have suggested that the peculiar "liberation theology" that preoccupied President Bush during at least part of his time in office was deeply counterproductive. "The way that President George W. Bush is making democracy promotion a central theme of his foreign policy has clearly contributed to the unease such efforts (and the idea of democracy promotion itself) are creating around the world," the Carnegie Endowment's Thomas Carothers wrote back in 2006.[53]

Others have gone further, suggesting that the very idea represents a deviation from George Washington's historic admonition that the country must "avoid foreign entanglements." "Why should the United States invest blood and treasure effecting regime change that could bring to power an anti-American populist—as happened when the kings and emperors fell in Egypt, Libya, Iraq, Iran, and Ethiopia?" conservative commentator Pat Buchanan has asked.[54]

The truth, however, is more complex. As the scholar Robert Kagan has eloquently pointed out, the United States has always been a "dangerous nation"—one with a tradition of promoting democratic principles beyond its borders that dates back to the earliest days of the republic.[55] And this mission has never been more urgent. In his 2005 State of the Union Address, President George W. Bush declared that the "best hope for peace in our world is the expansion of freedom in all the world."[56]

In the arena of democracy promotion, however, his administration failed to match its deeds to these words, and left office having stopped short of effecting the lasting changes in the Muslim world that are essential to our victory against the forces of radical Islam. President Obama now has an opportunity to succeed where his predecessor failed.

NOTES

1. White House, Office of the Press Secretary, *National Security Strategy of the United States of America*, September 2002, 7.

2. Arch Puddington, "Freedom in the World 2009: Setbacks and Resilience," in *Freedom in the World 2009* (Washington, DC: Freedom House, 2009), http://www.freedomhouse.org/uploads/fiw09/FIW09_OverviewEssay_Final.pdf.

3. Ibid.

4. An earlier version of this discussion appeared in the spring 2007 edition of *The Journal of International Security Affairs* under the title "The Death of Democracy Promotion?"

5. For an excellent explanation of the nexus between crime and democracy deficit, see Pavel Ivanov, "The (Not So) Untouchables," *The Journal of International Security Affairs* 10 (2006): 35–39.

6. President George W. Bush, address to the American Enterprise Institute, Washington, DC, February 26, 2003, http://www.whitehouse.gov/news/releases/2003/02/20030226-11.html.

7. See, for example, Secretary of State Condoleezza Rice, remarks at Princeton University's Celebration of the 75th Anniversary of the Woodrow Wilson School of Public and International Affairs, Princeton, New Jersey, September 30, 2005, http://www.state.gov/secretary/rm/2005/54176.htm.

8. Thomas Carothers, "Repairing Democracy Promotion," washingtonpost.com, September 14, 2007, http://www.washingtonpost.com/wp-dyn/content/article/2007/09/13/AR2007091302241.html.

9. Matt Kelley, "U.S. Money Helped Opposition in Ukraine," Associated Press, December 10, 2004.

10. Steven Woehrel, *Ukraine: Current Issues and U.S. Policy* (Washington, DC: Congressional Research Service, September 2008), 12–17.

11. See, for example, President George W. Bush, remarks on Winston Churchill and the War on Terror, Washington, DC, February 4, 2004, http://www.whitehouse.gov/news/releases/2004/02/20040204-4.html.

12. Thomas Carothers, "Promoting Democracy and Fighting Terror," *Foreign Affairs*, January/February 2003, http://www.foreignaffairs.org/20030101faessay10224/thomas-carothers/promoting-democracy-and-fighting-terror.html.

13. Vice President Dick Cheney, remarks at the 2006 Vilnius Conference, Vilnius, Lithuania, May 4, 2006, http://www.whitehouse.gov/news/releases/2006/05/20060504-1.html.

14. Daniel Pipes, "God and Mammon: Does Poverty Cause Militant Islam?" *The National Interest* 66 (2002): 14–21.

15. Ibid.

16. Lisa Curtis, "U.S. Aid to Pakistan: Countering Extremism through Education Reform," Heritage Foundation *Lecture* 1029, May 9, 2007, http://www.heritage.org/research/asiaandthepacific/hl1029.cfm.

17. C. Christine Fair, "Islamic Education in Pakistan," United States Institute of Peace trip report, 2006, 3.

18. U.S. House of Representatives, Republican Study Committee, "Pakistani Madrassa System and Foreign Students: Talking Points," n.d., http://www .house.gov/hensarling/rsc/doc/ca_071408_mccaulmadrassatwo.pdf.

19. Jeffrey Goldberg, "Inside Jihad U.; the Education of a Holy Warrior," *New York Times Magazine*, June 25, 2000, 32–42.

20. Ibid.

21. Former Pakistani Minister of Religious Affairs Mahmood Ahmed Ghazi, as cited in Lisa Curtis, "U.S. Aid to Pakistan: Countering Extremism through Education Reform," Heritage Foundation *Lecture* 1029, May 9, 2007, http:// www.heritage.org/research/asiaandthepacific/hl1029.cfm.

22. Caroline Cox and John Marks, *Islam, Islamism and the West: The Divide between Ideological Islam and Liberal Democracy* (Washington, DC: American Foreign Policy Council, 2005), 14–15.

23. For a more thorough discussion, see Bernard Lewis, *The Political Language of Islam* (Chicago: University of Chicago Press, 1988).

24. Mamoun Fandy, "Crisis of Education in the Muslim World," United States Institute of Peace *Fellow Project Report*, June 10, 2004, http://www.usip .org/fellows/reports/2004/0610_fandy.html.

25. *The Road not Traveled: Education Reform in the Middle East and North Africa* (Washington, DC: International Bank for Reconstruction and Development/The World Bank, 2008), 85.

26. Albert Kudsi-Zadeh, "Adult Education and the Challenge of Modernization in the Arab World: an Overview" European Association for Education of Adults, n.d., http://www.eaea.org/index.php?k=12091.

27. *The Road not Traveled: Education Reform in the Middle East and North Africa*, 96.

28. White House, Office of Management and Budget, "Report to Congress: United States Government Assistance Programs in Developing Countries for Basic Education," September 30, 2008 (author's collection).

29. Ibid.

30. Author's interview with Executive Branch official, Washington, DC, January 2009.

31. White House, Office of the Press Secretary, "Press Conference with President George W. Bush and Education Secretary Rod Paige to Introduce the President's Education Program," January 23, 2001, http://www.whitehouse .gov/news/releases/2001/01/20010123-2.html.

32. Judy Barsalou, "Islamists at the Ballot Box: Findings from Egypt, Jordan, Kuwait and Turkey," United States Institute of Peace *Special Report* 144 (2005), http://www.usip.org/pubs/specialreports/sr144.pdf.

33. As cited in David Schenker, ed. "Countering Islamists at the Ballot Box: Alternative Strategies," Washington Institute for Near East Policy *Policy Focus* 61 (November 2006): 12.

34. See, for example, Robert Leiken and Steven Brooke, "The Moderate Muslim Brotherhood," *Foreign Affairs* 86, no. 2 (2007): 107–21.

35. See, for example, "New Muslim Brotherhood Political Platform Bans Christians, Women from Presidency, Sets up Clerical Power," Associated Press, October 10, 2007, http://www.iht.com/articles/ap/2007/10/10/africa/ME-GEN-Egypt-Brotherhood-Platform.php.

36. As cited in Center for Special Studies, Intelligence and Terrorism Information Center, "Hezbollah," July 2003, http://www.intelligence.org.il/eng/bu/hizbullah/pb/app13.htm.

37. See, for example, Middle East Media Research Institute *Special Dispatch* 1048, December 13, 2005, http://memri.org/bin/articles.cgi?Page=countries&Area=turkey&ID=SP104805.

38. Statement by Abu Musab al-Zarqawi, as cited in James S. Robbins, "Al-Qaeda Versus Democracy," *The Journal of International Security Affairs* 9 (2005): 53.

39. "Muslim Brotherhood Movement Homepage," n.d., http://www.ummah.net/ikhwan/.

40. Prime Minister Recep Tayyip Erdogan, as cited in Middle East Media Research Institute *Special Dispatch* 1596, May 23, 2007, http://memri.org/bin/articles.cgi?Page=countries&Area=turkey&ID=SP159607.

41. See, for example, "Whither the Revolution or Wither the Revolution," Jewish Institute for National Security Affairs *JINSA Report* 575, June 2, 2006, http://www.jinsa.org/node/212.

42. See, for example, Joshua Muravchik, "Bomb Iran," *Los Angeles Times*, November 19, 2006, http://www.latimes.com/news/opinion/la-op-muravchik19nov19,0,1681154.story?coll=laopinion-center.

43. Office of the Director of National Intelligence, *National Intelligence Estimate: Iran: Intentions and Capabilities*, November 2007, http://www.dni.gov/press_releases/20071203_release.pdf.

44. Among these has been a simulation, carried out by the European Commission's Joint Research Centre in Ispra, Italy, in early 2008, which estimated that even if Iran's centrifuges work just a quarter of the time (25 percent efficiency), the Islamic Republic could generate enough fissile material for a nuclear weapon by the end of 2010. Markus Becker, "Alarming Test Results: Iran Could Have Enough Uranium for a Bomb by Year's End," *Der Spiegel* (Hamburg), February 21, 2008, http://www.spiegel.de/international/world/0,1518,536914,00.html. Other expert analyses have painted an even gloomier picture. According to a December 2008 study by the Washington, DC-based Institute for Science and International Security, Iran had already acquired roughly half the raw material for a nuclear weapon, and was estimated to be able to obtain the rest in a matter of months. As a result, the study concluded that "Iran is moving steadily toward this capability and is expected

to reach that milestone during 2009 under a wide variety of scenarios." David Albright, Jacqueline Shire, and Paul Brannan, "Has Iran Achieved a Nuclear Weapons Breakout Capability? Not yet, but Soon," Institute for Science and International Security *ISIS Report*, December 2, 2008, http://www.isisnucleariran .org/assets/pdf/LEU_Iran.pdf.

45. Morton M. Kondracke, "NIE's Upshot: War is Out, but Iran is Dangerous," *Roll Call*, December 6, 2007, http://www.rollcall.com/issues/53_67/kondracke/ 21232-1.html.

46. "Bush State of the Union Address," cnn.com, January 29, 2002, http:// archives.cnn.com/2002/ALLPOLITICS/01/29/bush.speech.txt/.

47. David M. Denehy, "The Iranian Democracy Imperative," *The Journal of International Security Affairs* 15 (2008): 97–103.

48. White House, Office of the Press Secretary, *National Security Strategy of the United States of America*, September 2002, 29.

49. Richard W. Stevenson, "Bush Appeals to Iran's Public in Radio Talk," *New York Times*, December 21, 2002, http://query.nytimes.com/gst/fullpage .html?res=9D0CEFD61E3DF932A15751C1A9649C8B63.

50. White House, Office of Management and Budget, "Iran All-Spigot Funding Chart," July 18, 2008. (author's collection)

51. In 2007, for example, the State Department chose to move $20 million earmarked specifically "to promote democracy in Iran" from its Middle East Partnership Initiative to the highly politicized Office of Iran Affairs—a decision that virtually guaranteed that the funds would not be effectively spent. Commenting on the move at the time, J. Scott Carpenter, a former Deputy Assistant Secretary for Near East Affairs, remarked wryly that "this pretty much kills the Iran democracy program." Eli Lake, "'This Pretty Much Kills the Iran Democracy Program,'" *New York Sun*, November 8, 2007, http://www.nysun .com/foreign/this-pretty-much-kills-the-iran-democracy-program/66065/.

52. See, for example, Adam Burke, "Video: Obama Outlines 'Surge of Diplomacy,'" *Iowa Independent*, September 13, 2007, http://iowaindependent .com/1007/video-obama-outlines-surge-of-diplomacy.

53. Thomas Carothers, "The Backlash against Democracy Promotion," *Foreign Affairs* 85, no. 2 (2006).

54. Patrick J. Buchanan, "What Does 'Democracy' Mean—Over There?" Creators Syndicate, May 2, 2005, http://wnd.com/index.php/index.php?fa=PAGE .printable&pageId=30117.

55. Robert Kagan, *Dangerous Nation: America's Foreign Policy from Its Earliest Days to the Dawn of the Twentieth Century* (New York: Alfred A. Knopf, 2006).

56. President George W. Bush, Inaugural Address, Washington, DC, January 20, 2005, http://www.whitehouse.gov/news/releases/2005/01/20050120-1 .html.

CONCLUSION

History, they say, has a way of repeating itself. Two decades ago, the world witnessed the largest totalitarian collapse in history with the breakup of the Soviet Union. The seeds of this breakdown were sown a decade earlier, when the Reagan administration abandoned the "cold peace" embraced by its predecessors and embarked upon a comprehensive national strategy to defeat the "evil empire."

But while America won that war, there can be little doubt that it failed to secure fully the peace that followed. Rather, enthralled by the idea that the collapse of the USSR had ushered in the "end of history" and the "universalization of Western liberal democracy as the final form of human government,"[1] the United States presided over a systematic dismantlement of the tools of its Cold War victory, from an unprecedented drawdown of its military power to the evisceration of its capacity to engage in strategic influence abroad.

Some, however, struck a more cautious note. In his famous 1993 treatise, the late, great political scientist Samuel Huntington warned that future conflicts may be defined as much by the fault lines between countries as the grievances among them.[2] Others had come to a similar conclusion. "We have slain a large dragon," the Clinton administration's incoming Director of Central Intelligence, R. James Woolsey, warned the Senate Select Committee on Intelligence during his confirmation hearing in February 1993. "But we live now in a jungle filled with a bewildering variety of poisonous snakes. And in many ways, the dragon was easier to keep track of."[3]

Fast-forward to the present, and that admonition turned out to have been positively prescient. Today, the United States confronts a new ideological adversary—one infinitely more implacable than the Soviet Union. And while America is not likely to embark on another holiday from international responsibility akin to the one that prevailed in the early 1990s, whether the Obama administration will continue to prosecute what has come to be known as the "long war" with the same vigor as its predecessor remains very much an open question.

It is one that our adversaries are actively pondering. In his January 2009 audio message, released just days before President Obama's inauguration, al-Qaeda leader Osama bin Laden wondered aloud whether, in his words, America "is capable to keep fighting us for more years."[4] From Tehran to Pakistan's Northwest Frontier Province, others are wondering very much the same thing.

How America answers them will make all the difference. In its final report on the atrocities of September 11, the National Commission on Terrorist Attacks Upon the United States, better known simply as the "9/11 Commission," famously concluded that one of the greatest failures of our fight against terrorism worldwide so far had been one of "imagination."[5]

Today, the United States has both the ability and the opportunity to correct this deficiency. Doing so requires building on the successes of the past eight years—from the start of a serious governmental effort to counterterrorism financing to a military mobilized for a protracted conflict—in order to reclaim the initiative on the dominant battlefields of today's conflict: ideology, strategic communications, economics, law, and development.

It is long past time for us to start.

NOTES

1. Francis Fukuyama, "The End of History?" *The National Interest* 16 (1989).

2. Samuel P. Huntington, "The Clash of Civilizations?" *Foreign Affairs* 72, no. 3 (1993): 22–49.

3. R. James Woolsey, testimony before the Senate Select Committee on Intelligence, Washington, DC, February 2, 1993.

4. Brian Ross, "Bin Laden Challenges Obama in New Audio Message," abcnews.com, January 14, 2009, http://abcnews.go.com/Blotter/story?id=6643641&page=1.

5. *The 9/11 Commission Report: Final Report of the National Commission on Terrorist Attacks Upon the United States* (New York: W.W. Norton, 2004), 339.

INDEX

Acheson, Dean, 32
Afghanistan: conditions in, xiii–xiv, 18; democracy promotion and, 93–95
Africa, and ideology, 25
Ahmadinejad, Mahmoud, 18, 62–65, 76
AKP (Justice and Development Party), 103–5
Al-Arabiya, 13
Al Barakat, 51
al-Hakaymah, Muhammad Khalil, 79
Al-Hayat, 12
Alhurra, 13, 36–37
Al-Jazeera, 13
allies, and ideological resistance, 23–26
Al-Manar, 12
alms, 59
al-Oudah, Salman, 14–15
al-Qaeda, xiii–xiv, 1, 25, 42; financial issues and, 51, 68; and ideology, 11–12, 14–16; leadership changes in, 7n5; metamorphosis of, xv, 2–3; and nature of conflict, 75–76
al-Qaradawi, Yusuf, 59

al-Shair, Abu Hazim, 7n5
al-Sharif, Sayyid, 14
Al-Sharq al-Awsat, 12
al-Thani, Hamad Khalifa, 13
al-Turabi, Hassan, 25–26
al-Zarqawi, Abu Musab, 79, 104
al-Zawahiri, Ayman, 2, 56
Annan, Kofi, 85
As-Sahab, 11
Atef, Mohammed, 7n5
Augustine, saint, 77

Baker, Gerard, xiv
banks, Iranian, 66–67
Baruch, Bernard, 69n4
Beers, Charlotte, 38
Bergen, Peter, 15–16
bin Laden, Osama, 1, 116; and ideology, 11–12, 14; metamorphosis of, 2; on nature of conflict, 75–76; on warfare, 79
bonyads, 63
Boykin, William, 12
British Petroleum, 62
broadcasting, history of, 33–36
Broadcasting Board of Governors, 34

Brohi, Allah Bukhsh K., 78
Brownback, Sam, 44
Buchanan, Pat, 109
Burns, Nicholas, 88
Bush, George W.: on axis of evil, 107;
    and education, 102; and United
    Nations, 87–88; and War on
    Terror, xiv–xv, 6
Bush administration: and
    citizen participation, 52; and
    counterterrorism, 1; and
    definitions of terrorism, 84; and
    democracy promotion, 93–95,
    98–99, 109; and divestment,
    70n13; and Iran, 61, 64; and Iraq,
    xiii; and media messaging, 36;
    and new way of war, 80–81; and
    public diplomacy, 48n21; and
    regime change, 106, 108

Carothers, Thomas, 98, 109
Carpenter, J. Scott, 113n51
Center for Security Policy, 37
Central Asia, and ideology, 23–25
Chaharshanbehsouri, 30n42
Cheney, Dick, 98–99
civilians, radical Islam on, 79
Cold War: financial mechanisms in,
    57; ideological messaging in, 31–50
combatants, definition of, 82
community, radical Islam on, 79
competition, market, and War on
    Terror, 55–58
Conflict Securities Advisory Group,
    69n10
counterterrorism, xiii–xvii, 1;
    democracy promotion and,
    93–113; economic issues
    and, 51–74; foreign aid and,
    56–57; identification of enemies
    in, xv, 1–9; ideology and,
    11–30; imagination and, 116;

international law and, 75–91;
    public diplomacy and, 31–50;
    United Nations and, 87
Cruickshank, Paul, 15–16
Cuba, 33
culture, Persian, Iran and, 20–21,
    29n42
Cyrus, king, 20

Darul Uloom Haqqania, 100
de Borchgrave, Arnaud, 5
Defense Science Board, 39–41, 44
democracy promotion, 93–113;
    elections and, 103–5; mechanisms
    of, 94–99; sustaining, 95–97
demographics: of Iran, 17; of Muslim
    world, 5, 101
Deobandi, 15
de Vittoria, Francisco, 77
divestment, 55, 70n13
Djerejian, Edward, 40
Doran, Michael Scott, 39
drug trade, and Iran, 18

economic issues: counterterrorism
    and, 51–74; and democracy
    promotion, 96; and education,
    101–2; global financial crisis,
    59, 65, 67–68; and Iran, 17–18;
    and Iraq, 3–4; post-Cold War
    cuts and, 33–35; and public
    diplomacy, 45, 48n21; and
    radicalization, 99–100; *sharia*
    and, 58–60
education, and democracy
    promotion, 99–103
Egypt, 25, 103
Eisenhower, Dwight D., 32
el-Bashir, Omar, 25
electoral politics, radical Islam and,
    103–5
enemies, identification of, xv, 1–9

Esposito, John, 5
European Recovery Program, 57

Fadl, Dr., 14
Fallon, William, 39
Faraj, Mohammed Abdel Salam, 78
Fatah, 97
Ferdowsi, Abolqasem, 21
financial crisis, global: Iran and, 65; opportunities in, 67–68; and *sharia* finance, 59. *See also* economic issues
foreign aid, and counterterrorism, 56–57
Foreign Assistance Act, 57
Friedman, Thomas, 65

gasoline supplies, Iran and, 60–63, 65
Gates, Robert, xvi, 3
Geneva Conventions, 76, 78, 80
Ghadir, 29n42
Gingrich, Newt, ix–x, 88
Glassman, James, 38
Global Islamic Media Front, 11
global security risk, internationalizing, 53–55
Grotius, Hugo, 78
Guantanamo Bay detention facilities, 81

Hague Conventions, 76, 78, 82
Hamas, 4, 82, 97
Hamdan, Salim Ahmed, 81
Harvard University, Islamic Finance Project, 59
Helms, Jesse, 91n40
Hezbollah, 3–4, 6, 12; and elections, 103–4; financial issues and, 56; Iran and, 20; status of, 82–84; and warfare, 79–80
Hoffer, Eric, 20

holidays, Persian, Iran and, 20–21, 29n42
Homeland Security Department, xiv
Hughes, Karen, 38
Huntington, Samuel, 115

ideology: and counterterrorism, 11–30; and messaging to Muslim world, 31–50
imagination, and counterterrorism, 116
India, 15, 72n46
information operations, 44
international law, 75–91
International Republican Institute, 96
international system, status quo view of, 77
Internet, in Middle East, 13
interrogation, 80–81
Iran: Bush on, 6; current state of, xv; defining opposition to, 3–5; financial issues and, 60–67; and ideology, 12, 17–23; and nuclear program, 19, 62, 112n44; regime change and, 106–8; and warfare, 79–80
Iraq, xiii, 2–4; democracy promotion and, 95; education in, 102; Oil-for-Food program and, 85–86; public diplomacy and, 39; regime change and, 106–7; surge strategy in, xiii, 95
Islam, radical: in Central Asia, state ideologies and, 23–25; defining enemies in, 1–9; democracy promotion and, 93–113; economic area denial and, 51–74; and education, 100–101; ideological offensive against, 11–30; international law and, 75–91; public diplomacy and, 31–50; and

warfare, 78–80; War on Terror and, xiii–xvii

Jaffari, Davoud Danesh, 66
Japan, 86–87
jihad, 79
jus ad bellum, 78
jus in bello, 78
Justice and Development Party, 103–5
just war doctrine, 77–78

Kagan, Robert, 109
Karzai, Hamid, 95
Kaveh the Blacksmith, 21
Kazakhstan, 23
Kennedy, John F., 57
Khalaji, Mehdi, 22
Khamenei, Ali, 4, 17
Khomeini, Ruhollah, 17, 21–22, 61
Kittrie, Orde, 62
Kondracke, Morton, 107
Kyrgyzstan, 23–24

Lajeunesse, Gabriel, 76
leadership, and public diplomacy, 44–45
Lebanon, 4, 20, 56, 103
Libya, 106
Lieberman, Joseph, 45
local governments, and ideology, 24
Lord, Carnes, 41
Lukoil, 54

Makram-Ebeid, Mona, 103–4
Malik, S. K., 78
market competition, and War on Terror, 55–58
Marshall Plan, 57
Mazaheri, Tahmasb, 67
McCain, John, 86
McCarthy, Andrew, 83

media: ideological offensive in, 11–30; message to Muslim world in, xv, 13, 31–50
Media Engagement Team, 39
Medvedev, Dmitry, 99
Middle East: dynamics of, issues in, 95; media in, 12–13
Middle East Free Trade Initiative, 93
Middle East Partnership Institute, 93, 113n51
Millennium Challenge Corporation, 93
Mogahed, Dalia, 5
Mohammed, Khalid, 7n5
Moore, Alan, 84
Moussaoui, Zacarias, 89n15
Murrow, Edward R., 34
Musharraf, Pervez, 98
Muslim Brotherhood, 42, 103–5
Muslim world: demographics of, 5, 101; identification and, 5–6; messaging to, xv, 13, 31–50. *See also* Islam: radical

National Commission on Terrorist Attacks Upon the United States, 116
National Defense Strategy, 2008, 1
National Democratic Institute, 96
nationalism, Iran and, 20–21, 29n42
National Security Act, xiv–xv
National Security Council, Paper 68, 32
National Security Decision Directives, 32–33
nation-state: radical Islamic view of, 78; Western view of, 76
Nigeria, 25
9/11 Commission, 116
No Child Left Behind, 102
noncombatants, radical Islam on, 79
non-state actors, and warfare, 76

North Korea, 107
Novikov, Evgueni, 24–25
nuclear programs: Iran and, 19, 62, 112n44; regime change and, 106–7

Obama, Barack: and divestment, 55; and Iran, 108; and warfare, 81
Office of Global Security Risk, 53–54
Office of Strategic Influence, 38–39
Oil-for-Food program, 85–86
Operation Green Quest, 51
Orange Revolution, 96

pacta sunt servanda, 77
Pakistan: democracy promotion and, 98; education in, 100–101; financial issues and, 56–57
Palestinian Authority, 97–98
Palestinian Islamic Jihad, 4
Pasdaran, 8n12, 63–64
Pattiz, Norman, 35
Petraeus, David, 39
Pipes, Daniel, 99
political approaches: al-Qaeda and, 16; Shi'ite Muslims and, 79–80; to War on Terror, xv–xvi
political campaigns, and public diplomacy, 42–43
political capacity-building, and democracy promotion, 97
poverty: in Africa, 25; in Iran, 18
President's Committee on International Information Activities, 32
Press TV, 12
prostitution, in Iran, 18
psychological operations, 32–33
public diplomacy, 31–50; campaign footing for, 42–43; offensive in, recommendations for, 40–41; reorganization for, 43–45
Putin, Vladimir, 99

Qassem, Naim, 4
Qutb, Sayyid, 42, 75

radical Islam. *See* Islam, radical
Radio Free Europe/Radio Liberty, 33
Radio Marti, 33
Radio Sawa, 36
Rafsanjani, Ali Akbar Hashemi, 63–64
Reagan, Ronald, 32–33, 66
regime change, 106–8
Reilly, Robert, 36
Reliance Industries, 72n46
religion: Iran and, 21–23; and state, Islam on, 104–5
Rice, Condoleezza, 61
Robbins, James S., 16
Ross, Dennis, 108
Rumsfeld, Donald, 39
Rusiya Al-Yaum, 13
Russia, democracy promotion and, 98–99

Salafism, 16
sanctions, and Iran, 64, 67
Saudi Arabia, 25, 46
Saxton, Jim, 6
Securities and Exchange Commission, 53
security risk, global, internationalizing, 53–55
self-determination movements, versus terrorism, 83
sharia finance, 58–60
Shariati, Ali, 61
Shi'ite Islam, 3; and political engagement, 21; and warfare, 79–80. *See also* Iran
Sistani, Ali, 22
Somalia, 25
State Department, 34, 37–38, 113n51

status quo view, of international
  system, 77
Stephens, Brett, 68
strategic influence, 31–50; definition
  of, 46n2; reorganization for, 43–45
Sudan, 25–26
Sunni Islam, xiii, 1; financial issues
  and, 56; Iran and, 4
Supreme Court, 81
Syria, 4, 90n38

Tajikistan, 23
Taleqani, Mahmoud, 61
Taliban, xiii
Talisman Energy, 54
Terror, War on. *See* War on Terror
terror-free investing, 54–55
terrorism: definitions of, 82–84;
  financial aspects of, 51–52;
  Iran and, 19–20; and warfare
  principles, 78–80. *See also* Islam:
  radical
Thirty Years' War, 76
Thomas Aquinas, saint, 77
torture, 80–81
Total, 62
Trafigura, 62
Truman, Harry, xiv–xv, 32
Turkey, 103–5
Turkmenistan, 23
Tutwiler, Margaret, 38

Ukraine, 96
umma, 79
unconventional warfare, 44
United Nations: Charter, 76–77, 83;
  critique of, 84–88

United States Agency for
  International Development
  (USAID), 57
United States Information Agency
  (USIA), 34, 43
Usmani, Muhammad Taqi, 59
Uzbekistan, 23–24

Vitol, 62
Voice of America, 33, 37
Volker, Paul, 85

Wahhabism, 16, 46
Waller, J. Michael, 41
warfare, 75–81; radical Islam and,
  78–80; Western principles of,
  76–78
War on Terror, xiii–xvii,
  115–16; citizens and, 52–53;
  identification of enemies in,
  xv, 1–9; nature of, 75–76;
  term, xv; widening, 6. *See also*
  counterterrorism
Washington, George, 109
waterboarding, 80
Western principles of warfare,
  76–78
Westphalia, Treaty of, 76–77
Wilson, Woodrow, 84
Woolsey, R. James, 58, 75, 115
Wunderle, William, 76

Yanukovych, Viktor, 96
Yushchenko, Viktor, 96

zakat, 59
Zubaidah, Abu, 7n5

ABOUT THE AUTHOR

Ilan Berman is vice president for policy of the American Foreign Policy Council in Washington, DC. An expert on regional security in the Middle East, Central Asia, and the Russian Federation, he has consulted for both the U.S. Central Intelligence Agency and the U.S. Department of Defense, and provided assistance on foreign policy and national security issues to a range of governmental agencies and congressional offices.

Mr. Berman is adjunct professor for international law and global security at the National Defense University and a member of the associated faculty at Missouri State University's Department of Defense and Strategic Studies. He also serves as a member of the reconstituted Committee on the Present Danger and as editor of *The Journal of International Security Affairs*.

Mr. Berman is the author of *Tehran Rising: Iran's Challenge to the United States* (Rowman & Littlefield, 2005), coeditor, with J. Michael Waller, of *Dismantling Tyranny: Transitioning Beyond Totalitarian Regimes* (Rowman & Littlefield, 2005), and—most recently—editor of *Taking on Tehran: Strategies for Confronting the Islamic Republic* (Rowman & Littlefield, 2007).